GOD'S LIVING WORD

GOD'S LIVING WORD

Biblical Virtues for Our Time

Rev. Paul Zilonka, C.P.

Illustrated

CATHOLIC BOOK PUBLISHING CO.
New York

IMPRIMI POTEST: Columkille Regan, C.P.
Provincial Superior

NIHIL OBSTAT: John Quinn, M.A.
Censor Librorum

IMPRIMATUR: Patrick J. Sheridan
Vicar General, Archdiocese of New York

The Nihil Obstat and Imprimatur are official declarations that a book or pamphlet is free of doctrinal or moral error. No implication is contained therein that those who have granted the Nihil Obstat and Imprimatur agree with the contents, opinions or statements expressed.

The Scripture quotations are taken from the *New American Bible with Revised New Testament* copyright © 1986 by the Confraternity of Christian Doctrine, Washington, DC. Used with its permission. All rights reserved.

(T-146)

© 1990 Catholic Book Publishing Co., N.Y.
Printed in the U.S.A.

CONTENTS

Preface 9

THE SEARCH FOR GOD

Noah: The Waters of Life 15
Abraham: Respect for Life 17
Jonah: Compassion for Sinners 20
Lady Wisdom: The Gifts of Life 22
Micah: Moral Courage 24
Ezekiel: Hope for the Depressed 27
The Magi: Finding God 29
The Penitent Woman: Obtaining Forgiveness . 31
The Rich Man: Freedom from Possessions 34
Martha: Loving Concern 36
Zacchaeus: True Conversion 38
Mary Magdalene: A New Life 40
Judas: Compassion and Consolation 43
Paul: Authentic Zeal 45

COVENANT LIFE AND LOVE

Joshua: Upholding Tradition 50
Ruth: Undying Fidelity 52
Solomon: Wisdom without Love 54
Hosea: God's Enduring Love 57

James and John: Worldly Ambition 59
Friends of a Paralytic: Commitment to Jesus . 62
The Poor Widow: A Generous Heart 64
The Stooped Woman: Religious Hypocrisy 66
The Good Shepherd: Searching for the Sheep . 69
The Prodigal Son: Showing Compassion 71
The Disciples of Emmaus: Redemptive
   Suffering 73
Thomas: Unwavering Faith 76
Stephen: Serving God's Community 78
Lydia: Apostolic Women 81
Prisca and Aquila: Dedicated Laity 83

ANNOUNCING THE GOOD NEWS

Jesus of Nazareth: Bearer of Good News 89
Qoheleth: The Perplexity of Life 94
Rahab: Faith Commitment 96
Amos: Love for the Poor 99
Isaiah: Peace with Justice 101
Jeremiah: Preaching the Word of God 104
Susanna: Perseverance in Virtue 106
Second Isaiah: Proclaiming the Good News . 109
John the Baptist: Bearing Witness 111
The Widow of Nain: Life out of Death 114

Simeon: Hope for the Future	116
Andrew: Leading Others to Christ	118
The Samaritan Woman: Sharing Christ with Others	121
Peter: Denial of Christ	123
Nicodemus: Light out of Darkness	125
Conclusion	128

PREFACE

MANY learned and successful people look upon the Bible as little more than one giant script for the religious drama department of a Hollywood movie studio, or the blueprint for a Disney World style religious theme park complete with a ride on Noah's Ark or a parachute jump from the top of an imitation Mt. Sinai! For those of us who esteem the Bible as a privileged body of literature reflecting the faith of Jews and Christians of ancient times, and gathered together under the inspiration of the Holy Spirit, this secularist evaluation is not true.

The Bible has not always been served well by the Hollywood moguls. But much could be said as well about the disservice rendered it by the ministers of the Church over the centuries. People who live in glass houses should think twice before casting the first stone.

A religious theme park might have the exemplary goal of bringing biblical characters to life by using authentic costumes and recreating dramas and displays of biblical stories. But the people inside the costumes are still twentieth-century people. At the end of the working day, they jump into their cars and plunge back into the modern world on the congested highway. They never really left the modern world. They cannot and should not leave it! The present moment is where we are meant to live.

The people of the Bible were real people, just like us—flesh, blood, feelings, hopes, loves, successes, and failures. They were the product of their environment as much as we are. If they were transported in a time machine into the present, they might not be able to cope with the changes. But the same could be said of us, if we were suddenly transported to ancient Jerusalem or Babylon. Modern studies in archeology and sociology try to enlighten us on the worldview and ordinary experiences of ancient biblical peoples. As might be expected, the differences can be enormous. This should alert us to the dangers of a simplistic literal imitation of their actions or words.

Yet, many of the words and deeds of biblical people are indeed timeless and equally valid for our day as they were for them. The following reflections wish to focus on those similarities, so that the stories we read of these biblical people might influence us in our own search for holiness.

Truth in the Bible is set forth and expressed differently in texts that are historical, prophetic, poetic, or make use of other types of contemporary literary forms appropriate to that time and culture. The sacred writers did not have a strictly biographical scope in reporting the names and events associated with these many biblical personalities. Most often they probably had little or no biographical information, and rarely personal experience of the people in question. Contemporary Gospel study has shown that lack of strictly biographical interest is even true in regard to Jesus. Almost all of the biographical data about Jesus that we might glean from the Gospels is usually deduced from allusions and references to other people and events, for whom we have some source of information different from the Bible.

These brief reflections do not intend to do what the evangelists and other sacred authors did not intend! They are simply thoughts inspired by the Scriptures that hope to allow the biblical message to come through clearly and honestly, yet with a touch of sensitivity to the humanness of the biblical personages. We are always in the situation of the biblical theme park. We can know the stories of the real and imaginary people of the biblical world, but we remain people of the twentieth century. However, the stories of these biblical characters can be the instruments of God in fashioning a twentieth-century community, just as they have been influential in past centuries. This little collection hopes to be a small contribution to that work of the Holy Spirit in our own day.

THE SEARCH
FOR
GOD

NOAH
The Waters of Life

"This is the sign that I am giving for all ages to come, of the covenant between me and you and every living creature with you. I set my bow in the clouds to serve as a sign of the covenant between me and the earth" (Genesis 9:12-13).

THE story of Noah and the ark is one of those Bible tales that make a great deal of sense to us when we are young. It has action and adventure, the triumph of good over evil, a menagerie of animals to keep our childhood imaginations entertained for hours, and, what's most important, a happy ending with a beautiful rainbow.

When we grow up, we often replace our childish delight with what we consider to be common sense. We get serious about life. We stop chasing rainbows because we know there will be no pot of gold at the end. However, it is when we have "come to our senses" and get on with the business of life that we most need to read again the story of Noah—not as a primer in zoology, but as a story of sin and grace.

The worldwide deluge of the Hebrew scriptures bears striking resemblance to similar flood stories in the literature of other ancient cultures. This is particularly true of the Gilgamesh Epic, which Jewish deportees encountered in Babylon during their captivity there some 500 years before the birth of Christ.

Yet the amazing similarities found in all these ancient stories only serve to highlight the significant difference in the Genesis version of the flood. The pagan stories usually picture the flood as the erratic whim of a disgruntled god. However, Genesis lays the blame squarely on the shoulders of the human race when it says that God's heart was grieved when he saw human wickedness and "how no desire that [the human] heart conceived was ever anything but evil" (Genesis 6:5).

Noah and his family were providentially saved through the ark because Noah found favor with the Lord. God established a covenant with him and with the renewed earth, because he had lived a righteous life in the midst of a perverse people. After the cataclysmic destruction of the flood, God renewed his earlier command to "be fertile and multiply and fill the earth" (Genesis 8:17).

Water still brings devastation in our own days. It terrifies and kills. Yet it also nourishes the crops and enables all life to survive. The rainbow after a storm can still serve to turn our thoughts to the Lord who is the source of all life.

The New Testament rightly interpreted the story of Noah in which eight people were saved as a prefigurement of Christian Baptism through which innumerable others would be saved for life eternal. This salvific water is "not a removal of dirt from the body but an appeal to God for a clear conscience, through the resurrection of Jesus Christ, who has gone into heaven and is at the right hand of God, with angels, authorities, and powers subject to him" (1 Peter 3:21-22).

Prayer

LORD, thank you for the waters of Baptism that have given me life in your Spirit. Accompany me all the days of my life with your love so that I may remain faithful to you.

☆ ☆ ☆

ABRAHAM
Respect for Life

"Take your son Isaac, your only one, whom you love, and go to the land of Moriah. There you shall offer him up as a holocaust on a height that I will point out to you" (Genesis 22:2).

IN church we frequently hear the selection of Genesis 12 in which God calls Abraham to leave his homeland for the land to the south which God intends to give as an inheritance to Abraham's children. Although Abraham had no children at the time, he obeyed God. In time, Isaac, the son of promise, was born.

The implication of all this for the reader is fairly straightforward. We should also obey God when he calls us to something new, even though we may not see how it will be accomplished. It is all very comforting. It is also very safe to stop reading Abraham's story at this point.

What shall we say about the terrifying sequence to all of this? The same God who gave the miracle child tells Abraham to put him to death. For three days, the little group of Abraham, Isaac, and two servants journeyed to the mountain, which in sacred tradition is the Temple mount at Jerusalem. On the third day, Abraham took the wood for the fire from the donkey and laid it on the shoulders of his son Isaac, while he himself carried the fire and the knife. The Hebrew storyteller plunges a knife of sorrow into us as we listen to Isaac ask his father where they will get the animal for sacrifice. Abraham answers that God will provide.

Again there is a contemporary application. It is relatively easy to make some changes in life, as Abraham did when he left his father's house, if we know there is a reward for making the sacrifice involved. But, in this further incident, Abraham's fidelity remained just as spontaneous when God's heart-rending command touched the child of Abraham's old age, the child through whom God intended to fulfill his original promise of blessing.

But we rebel against the image of God as such a cruel tyrant. Even to call it a test of Abraham's faith does not really soothe our deeply felt complaint that this kind of God cannot be worthy of our love. What kind of God would torture an old man in such a way?

We should not try to suppress these thoughts because they actually enable God's revelation to take root in us. When the people of Israel took up residence in Canaan, they found entrenched there false religions that practiced infant sacrifice to appease the gods. The Israelites felt a revulsion toward that practice, which you and I feel when we read this story. They knew that human life was a most precious gift of God. He would never command such deeds. Instead, through this tradition of Abraham, the Israelites understood a divine command to offer an animal as a sign of their fidelity, while still preserving and respecting the gift of human life.

Today, the false gods still demand their offerings. Too many people are ready to sacrifice their children, whether through neglect and lack of diligent education or even through abortion. These parents sacrifice the welfare of their children for the momentary gratification of a life of ease and convenience. They worship at the shrine of comfort and independence that is only a mask for selfishness.

Prayer

GOD, creator of all women and men, deepen our respect for the seamless garment of human life from its first moment to the last breath. Make us particularly sensitive for the welfare of those who are weak and powerless.

JONAH
Compassion for Sinners

"Set our for the great city of Nineveh, and preach against it; their wickedness has come up before me" (Jonah 1:2).

SEVERAL hundred years before the birth of Jesus, a biblical writer with keen insight into human foibles composed the story of Jonah and the great fish. He used the admittedly fantastic tale in order to speak of God's universal love for all people, as well as the narrowness that sometimes afflicts the ministers of God's salvation. Jonah was reluctant at first to get involved with God. "Reluctant" is too tame a word to describe Jonah's attempt to escape by booking on a ship headed in the exact opposite direction from the overland journey to Nineveh! However, Jonah discovered that God is not so easily fooled.

He soon found himself back at his starting point, thanks to the fish. This time he did seem to get into the swing of it. After all, he was not preaching God's retribution against the people of Israel. Nineveh had been the capital of Assyria—an empire that had put the word "atrocity" in the dictionary of warfare. Though it had been reduced to rubble in 609 B.C., long before our author composed the tale of Jonah, the mere mention of that capital had become synonymous with wickedness, like Sodom and Egypt.

The author of this didactic novel portrays a Jonah who really hopes the Ninevites will suffer God's vengeance to every last man, woman, and child. The prophet is perplexed when the king of Nineveh and all its people don sackcloth (in good Jewish fashion) and proclaim a fast after only one day's worth of preaching. A preacher genuinely interested in his congregation's salvation would certainly jump for joy at such a dramatic turn of events. God was pleased so much that he called off the catastrophe. But Jonah was angry, a clear case of the prophet's prejudice getting in the way of his message of salvation.

So God teaches him a lesson in the way God often does, through a parable that at first seems unrelated to the point of the matter. God provides a wide-leafed plant to shade Jonah from the scorching sun. But the next day God sends a worm to destroy the plant. This little development is enough to send Jonah into another paroxysm. But God makes his point (as the spokesman for the author), "You are concerned over the plant which cost you no labor. . . . Should I not be concerned over Nineveh, the great city, in which there are more than a hundred and twenty thousand persons who cannot distinguish their right hand from their left?" (Jonah 4:10).

We and Jonah are left with that sober question. God created every person and does not rejoice in the unrepentant death of anyone. This is not an easy biblical truth to proclaim in societies where violence of all types is constantly perpetrated against innocent victims. The primal urge to vindictive retribution is strong. It is a lot easier to ramble on about whether Jonah was really inside a whale, than it is to face the hard truth that God is more forgiving than we are. The Book of Jonah is not a fairy tale for children, but a truth serum for adults.

Prayer

LORD God, you are rich in mercy toward sinners. Give us a compassionate spirit, especially toward those who have harmed us in any way so that our anger will be healed.

LADY WISDOM
The Gifts of Life

"Come, eat of my food, and drink of the wine I have mixed!" (Proverbs 9:5).

TELEVISION commercials occasionally present a romantic scene of a man and a woman sharing a dinner by candlelight, toasting each other with bubbling champagne in fine crystal glasses. It is the perfect advertising scene for selling champagne at New Year's or diamond necklaces anytime. The setting portrays elegance. Its clear message to prospective customers is class, distinction, and worldly success. Agencies use it because it is effective. Since the Bible arose out of human experience, it should not surprise us to read of a similar scene in the Book of Proverbs that has all the contemporaneity of this modern commercial.

Lady Wisdom, the handmaid of God, builds an elegantly decorated house. Then, she prepares a banquet of delicious meat and fine wines with all the trimmings. She sends her housemaids out with an invitation, and she herself calls from the highest part of the city so that all below would be sure to hear. She beckons to the simple and those lacking understanding to learn from her, to nourish themselves with the food and drink of wisdom that she offers.

Lady Wisdom minces no words when it comes to the facts of life. Ignoring her can only lead to death.

This is a strong statement that is visualized in a similar scene further along in which Lady Folly sits at the doorway of her house calling to passersby. "Stolen water is sweet and bread gotten secretly is pleasing" (Proverbs 9:17). Lady Folly has many names. She is a dope pusher promising a "high." She is a "fence" selling stolen television sets in a ghetto parking lot. Lady Folly is the vast cult of consumerism that creates such materialistic expectations in people of modest means that they sometimes resort to wrongdoing, or at least they do harm to themselves, to attain such things. Lady Folly supports "safe" sex without commitment or responsibility, white lies for self-advancement, and promises without honesty.

The two Ladies invite us to sit at their table, to feast on what they offer. In both cases, there is a price to pay—not at the entrance but upon tasting the meal. After we have dined with Lady Folly, we discover too late that her guests—ourselves included—are among the dead.

But Lady Wisdom also exacts a price for her generosity. She never allows us to go back to mediocrity with an easy conscience. She knows that once we have tasted her divine nourishment, that which alone on this earth can satisfy our desire, we will long for more and forsake Lady Folly's enticing call.

Prayer

LORD, send your spirit of divine wisdom into my heart, that I may alway know which path to choose, and that I may have the courage to follow it.

MICAH
Moral Courage

"You have been told . . . what is good and what the Lord requires of you: only to do the right and to love goodness, and to walk humbly with your God" (Micah 6:8).

NOVELISTS, poets, and even anonymous fables about country mouse and city mouse, have often caricatured the difference between city dwellers and citizens of rural districts. The contrast often portrays the former group as sophisticated and progressive, while the residents of the countryside are usually described as uneducated, conservative, and even morally suspect. Modern

MICAH: MORAL COURAGE

literary criticism might well suppose that such tendencies betray the bias of their authors who appear to be thoroughly citified!

Micah of Moresheth, a district some twenty miles southwest of Jerusalem, certainly qualifies as a man of rural background and conservative convictions. However, that is as far as he conforms to the proverbial caricature of a "country bumpkin." He seems to have been an elderly spokesman for his neighbors, small farmers who had tilled their family plots on the rolling hills looking westward to the Mediterranean for centuries from one generation to the next.

While men like Micah solidly supported the kings of Judah who ruled by right of God's promise to David, they had less sympathy for the bureaucratic underlings who were expropriating farm lands from under the feet of their residents through new land surveys, foreclosures on debts, forced slavery, bribery, and false weights and measures.

Likewise, the immoral behavior of so many Jerusalemites made the priestly emphasis on the atoning power of animal sacrifice seem quite hypocritical. Micah may have been born in the country, but he made a big noise in Jerusalem on more than one occasion. Naturally, his opponents, the king's official advisors, told him to go home and stop disturbing "the peace." His answer to that was, "Thus says the Lord regarding the prophets who lead my people astray; who when their teeth have something to bite, announce peace, but when one fails to put something in their mouth proclaim war against him. Therefore, you shall have night and not vision, darkness not divination ... because there is no answer from God" (Micah 3:5-7).

Naturally, Micah's public criticism of the government and religious establishment did not endear him to the groups targeted by him as chief offenders. He was very much an eighth-century-B.C. enthusiast of the twentieth-century philospy that "small is beautiful." Jerusalem's elite classes had forgotten the humbleness of their origins and the real power behind the throne. So God would start over again with another David. "You, Bethlehem-Ephrathah, too small to be among the clans of Judah, from you shall come forth for me one who is to be ruler in Israel" (Micah 5:1). The city folks were too caught up in securing their comfortable life-style at the expense of the country districts.

Micah can be pardoned for losing his temper over an issue that deeply involved him. Indeed, he spoke with the convictions that God was using him to shatter the false "peace" of those who were lulled into moral complacency by the official, state-approved prophets up on Capitol Hill! Micah proclaimed a different kind of future with a ruler who shall "shepherd his flock by the strength of the Lord . . . [and whose] greatness shall reach to the ends of the earth; he shall be peace" (Micah 5:3-4).

Prayer

L ORD Jesus, we acclaim you as son of David, good shepherd, prince of universal peace!

EZEKIEL
Hope for the Depressed

"Our bones are dried up, our hope is lost, and we are cut off" (Ezekiel 37:11).

DURING my travels to several world capitals, I have often asked taxi drivers if they think there are more bad people or good people in the world. I would expect them to say "more good people by far," which is what I believe. Many of the drivers have agreed, but I was often shocked at how many did not agree with my optimism. I realized that the pessimistic view always came from those who worked the night shift. These men spoke of their disgust with some of the people they had to transport during the night, people whose main goals in life seemed to center on alcohol and sexual libertinism. This little survey brought home to me once again how our perception of life is very much conditioned by the kind of experience we have.

Ezekiel was an Old Testament prophet with a difficult mission. During the Babylonian Exile, he listened to the pessimistic comments of his fellow Israelites day in and day out. As far as they were concerned, there were far more bad people in the world than good ones, and all the bad ones had their sandals upon the shoulders of the exiles! Ezekiel's compatriots thought of themselves as walking skeletons without breath, without beauty, without the laughter and delight of smiling faces. "By the streams of Babylon, we sat and wept when we remembered Zion.... How could we sing a song of the Lord in a foreign land?" (Psalm 137:1-4).

Ezekiel's companions were very angry. They had reason to be angry because their Babylonian conquerors had carted them off hundreds of miles from Judah and inducted them into government service and agricultural projects. But they were also angry for bringing this catastrophe upon their own heads. The prophets had railed loud and long that Judah could not give lip-service to Yahweh, while putting all their hopes on other deities and more "practical" types of security. They had to learn the hard way that the person who trusts in material wealth or who worships the products of one's own hands has little grounds for complaint when these tenuous security blankets fail as a life-threatening illness comes, or when the rich man finds himself abandoned by his "friends" who sense the tide of his bank account shifting downward.

When anger turns in against oneself, depression strikes hard. Because our experiences condition our perception of the world, Ezekiel found himself in the midst of an angry, depressed people. His message to them did not gloss over the dejection that sapped their human spirit. His prophetic vision led him through a valley of dry bones, but he was not reduced to silence. Rather, the Lord directed him to speak: "Thus says the Lord God to these bones: See! I will bring spirit into you that you come to life" (Ezekiel 37:5). And even as he prophesied, he saw the bones come together. Sinew and flesh came upon them, and finally spirit came and they stood upright, a vast army.

Whether it be taxi drivers on the night shift or exiles embittered by oppression and self-hatred, there are a lot of depressed people in the world. The Lord's message through prophets like Ezekiel is one of hope and restoration of what is good and true. Though it may not be obvious to those in the depression, the prophet's words are worthy of trust.

Prayer

LIGHTEN our darkness, Lord, with the vision of your prophets!

THE MAGI
Finding God

"And you, Bethlehem, land of Judah, are by no means least among the rulers of Judah; since from you shall come a ruler, who is to shepherd my people Israel" (Matthew 2:6).

DETECTIVE novels often prove that even the most clever murderers can make some dumb mistakes that lead to their arrest. The Bible has its share of murderers. Herod (called "The Great") was king in Israel when Jesus was born. Herod might have been king, but he made a few big mistakes.

Matthew's Gospel describes Herod and the whole city of Jerusalem as "greatly troubled" at the inquiry of the magi about the birthplace of the newborn king of Israel. Herod was not amused by this reference to a new king since he was extremely suspicious of the ambitions of several of his sons whom he eventually executed to secure his own peaceful sleep for a few more nights.

The irony of all this is that Herod was no stranger to murder. He could easily have dispatched his soldiers to deal with this latest threat to his oppressive dictatorship. Instead, he decided to use the magi to lead him to the victim child. "When you have found him," he said, feigning piety, "bring me word, that I too may go and do him homage" (Matthew 2:8).

Poor old Herod! He must have felt smug as he sent them on their way. But he underestimated God—if he even believed in God. When he let the magi walk away without a stakeout team to follow them, he was letting Jesus slip through his fingers. One of the biggest murderers in the Bible thus shows himself to be just as susceptible to stupidity as the rest of us.

What is more important than Herod's mental lapse was that the magi did find their newborn king. They prostrated themselves and did him homage. They then opened their treasures and offered him gifts of gold, frankincense, and myrrh.

This whole story is filled with symbolism, for the magi were astrologers who specialized in discerning the destiny of their clients for a handsome sum, weaving their incantations in incense-filled rooms and writing their advice with quill pen and myrrh.

How clever Matthew is in showing the complete subordination of these pagans to the newborn king! This gesture symbolizes what will indeed be the future development of Christian faith among the Gentiles. Herod, on the other hand, even with his scholarly biblical advisors, remains in the dark. Even his consequent vicious bloodletting of the Bethlehem infants cannot stop God's plan.

Finding God in today's world is not always the prerogative solely of those who have the "Sacred Scriptures." The story of the magi clearly demonstrates how God can be found by people of goodwill who take the Scriptures to heart and find the Lord through them. Too many people are like Herod who could have found life, but instead only sowed death in his path.

Prayer

L ORD, hold back the hand of those who would bring death on their neighbors, particularly the innocent and the defenseless. Convert the heart of all who embrace violence.

THE PENITENT WOMAN
Obtaining Forgiveness

"Now there was a sinful woman in the city who learned that he was at table in the house of the Pharisee. Bringing an alabaster flask of ointment, she stood behind him at his feet weeping and began to bathe his feet with her tears" (Luke 7:37-38).

THE woman came in by the back door, the servant's entrance. She was accustomed to arriving and departing quietly, without attracting attention to herself, avoiding suspicious housewives who had good reason to question their husband's fidelity. She moved easily in the midst of men, because she had looked many in the eye, close-up. She knew well how to measure the depth of a man's soul by looking intently in his eyes.

A lot of men delighted in looking at her. They were anxious to romance her in secret, but they all looked away when she saw them in daylight, in the town market, or at the door of their shops.

She had learned early in life that the cards were stacked against her. She was a person in a society where even the sacred law of the Almighty (Blessed be he!) was weighted against her simply because she had the unlucky fate of being born a woman.

But this man Jesus was not like the others. He had nothing to fear from her, no past encounters to hide. He was not afraid to look in her eyes from the moment she entered the room. He did not recoil from her despite the murmurs and vulgar remarks that circled the dining room of Simon's house as she stopped at the foot of the couch on which Jesus reclined.

She had heard him speak of the Father's love, and in those words she sensed something pure and strengthening, something that brought joy and healing to her battered heart. Those thoughts unleashed a flood of grateful love within her. Of all God's creatures, only a human being can laugh and cry. Her love brought the tears saved up from a thousand nights of pretense and frustration, the tears of a thousand memories all crushed together within her aching head that no one ever seemed to notice. And even if they had noticed, who would have cared?

But he cared. He perceived, this sensitive one whose whole bearing and the words he spoke awakened in her the certitude that her life could be different, that she could be free of those demeaning relationships, that forgiveness can heal forever, and even that the God whom she had feared as a judge all her life was not really just like one more male oppressor.

All her tears had been meaningless until now. How often she had felt like the refuse of crushed grape skins left behind in the winepress at harvest time. But this night, her tears could cleanse and refresh his tired and dusty feet. Without saying a word, those tears spoke her deepest feelings as if to say what Charles de Foucauld would pray to the heavenly Father centuries later: "I love you, Lord, and so need to give myself, to surrender myself into your hands, without reserve, and with boundless confidence, for you are my Father."

Prayer

L ORD Jesus, your words awaken grateful love and confidence within me. Help me to entrust myself into the hands of your Father and my Father with readiness to live the truth in love.

THE RICH MAN
Freedom from Possessions

"Jesus, looking at him, loved him and said to him, 'You are lacking in one thing. Go, sell what you have, and give to the poor and you will have treasure in heaven; then come, follow me' " (Mark 10:21).

MODERN business advertising spends a great deal of money and artistic creativity convincing prospective customers that the sponsor's product will bring happiness, security, love, or whatever else the consumer presently lacks. The underlying message is that if you own this product, your worries are over. In many cases, this is not an empty promise. However, the unwary consumer may eventually discover that possessions control rather than serve us docilely.

The rich man in the Gospel story discovered to his dismay that his material possessions could not fulfill the deepest yearning of his heart. He was a pious Jew who could humbly claim lifelong fidelity to the Ten Commandments given to Moses on Sinai. Yet he searched for more depth in his religious experience. He came to Jesus and asked the right questions. "What must I do to inherit eternal life?" (Mark 10:17).

The Gospel narrative is so poignant when it says that Jesus looked at him and loved him. How the man must have sensed that love! But the joy on both their faces was abruptly frozen and melted away when Jesus answered the loved one's question. It was too radical. Jesus was asking too much.

The invitation of Jesus had struck against the wall with which the rich man had insulated himself. Sadly, he discovered that he could not escape from the fortress his wealth had constructed around him.

He had walked up to the brink of eternity, only to discover that his material possessions would not let go of him. Teresa of Avila wrote that when the Lord draws us to himself, we must fly to him as a bird soars from the earth to a distant treetop. But if the bird is tied to the earth, it matters little whether it is by a tiny string or a heavy chain. In either case, the Lord's invitation cannot be accepted.

We may not be weighted down with material wealth as was the rich man in this story. Yet we might be frustrated in our love relationship with the Lord because of the multitude of seemingly insignificant possessions, or the spirit of possessiveness itself, that keeps us firmly rooted in mother earth and pinning our hopes on this world alone.

Jokes are sometimes made that one never sees a Brink's Security truck behind a hearse on the way to the cemetery. But Job has said it best. "Naked I came forth from my mother's womb, and naked shall I go back again" (Job 1:21). If we do not use possessions with discretion, they will bury us long before we die.

Prayer

L ORD, you know how often my possessions possess me. Free me from this modern slavery so that I may go where you invite me and do what you ask. In this way alone can I find my true happiness in this life.

☆   ☆   ☆

MARTHA
Loving Concern

"Lord, do you not care that my sister has left me by myself to do the serving?" (Luke 10:40).

MUCH-MALIGNED Martha! So many who carry her name mention, half with a smile but also half-seriously, the unfair treatment she received from Jesus. They say that after he chided her for thinking only of the kitchen and trying to interfere with Mary's "better" choice of sitting at Jesus' feet for a good conversation, you can be sure that he sat down to a delicious dinner that would not have been there without Martha's generous concern.

Concern and loving care, yes, Jesus wants us to show these to others. But anxiety, no. He is clear about that. "Martha, Martha, you are anxious and worried about many things" (Luke 10:41).

Anxiety might seem to be a particularly modern illness. It certainly gets a great deal of press. But it is hardly new on the human scene. The Gospels tackle it straight on. It ought not to be in the life of the Christian if priorities are correct and spiritual helps are being used.

Of course, parents will have sleepless nights worrying about their sick children; young adults will nervously await exam results that will determine their chances of obtaining one of the few places available in certain schools. Since the joys and hopes, the griefs and anxieties of the people of this age are shared totally by Christians, they will be anxious at times. But this anxiety arises out of genuine concern. Paul the Apostle spoke of his own daily burden of concern for the churches he had founded.

The kind of anxiety that Jesus cannot endure is that which arises out of misplaced priorities and abusive endeavors; the sleepless nights that are the result of a life-style dictated by the search for pleasure rather than sacrifice; the tangle of questionable relationships that more often than not postpone a generous surrender to the Gospel call to holiness.

Jesus loved Martha as much as Mary. He certainly did enjoy a good meal because of Martha's loving care. But his admonition remains as true today as it was then. We need to have loving care without anxious preoccupation. Listening to Jesus goes hand in hand with such care and keeps us from losing sight of the balance Christ intends for us under the Father's providential care.

Prayer

L ORD, transform our worldly anxiety into a care born of Gospel charity. May we be generous in service, and always peaceful in our hearts.

ZACCHAEUS
True Conversion

"Today salvation has come to this house because this man too is a descendant of Abraham. For the Son of Man has come to seek and to save what was lost" (Luke 19:9-10).

THE Gospels do not indulge our curiosity about the weight or height of Jesus. However, in the story of Zacchaeus, the evangelist Luke does make a point of saying that this tax collector was short in stature. Of course, this explains why Jesus had to invite him to "come down quickly" from his perch in the sycamore.

The townspeople of Jericho were surprised, but certainly Zacchaeus must have been the most surprised of all. As tax collector, he was not accustomed to any "Good morning" wave or "Good evening, sir" greeting from his neighbors. It is one thing to collect taxes for one's own government; it is quite another to do this work for an oppressive colonial regime backed up by military troops.

Jesus recognized Zacchaeus for what he was first of all, a descendant of Abraham. Jesus was seeking the lonely and lost. He had a special love for those who were materially poor but spiritually rich in many ways. At the same time, he did not abandon those wealthy in material possessions, because he knew they were often most needy of spiritual care.

ZACCHAEUS: TRUE CONVERSION

The crowd was not impressed with Jesus' preferential treatment of the mousy little tax collector whose collaboration with Rome enabled him to line his own pockets with profits skimmed from the regular duties paid by local residents. They grumbled as people often do when they think an ingrate has been preferred at the expense of their goodness. Grumbling never seemed to prevent Jesus from following through on his own agenda. He was searching for lost sheep with a persistence that could not tolerate such hurt feelings that arose more from self-pity than from genuine concern for the salvation of all people.

Jesus' loving choice to stay at Zacchaeus' house had its desired effect. Conversion, that is, learning to walk in a new way, took place that day. Once a person has met Christ, there is no telling what changes can begin to occur. "Behold, half of my possessions, Lord, I shall give to the poor, and if I have extorted anything from anyone I shall repay it four times over" (Luke 19:8). Zacchaeus was not only recommitting himself to the sacred Jewish legal tradition of a thief restoring fourfold to someone he had victimized. He went even further with a dramatic fifty percent tithe of all his assets with the proceeds going to the poor.

Jesus often spoke of the difficulty of rich people coming to enjoy his kingdom because their material possessions would so encumber their spirit that they could not revel in the values of that kingdom. After all, that is like expecting a camel to pass through the eye of a needle!

Yet this is one of those kingdom success stories in which the camel sheds its superfluous baggage and inches through the needle's eye to the amazement—and it seems the consternation—of the bystanders who would have denied Zacchaeus his grace-filled meeting with the Galilean prophet. Do we help the rich meet Christ, or merely stand by, both envious of their wealth and miserly in our prayer for them?

Prayer

LORD, you were rich and became poor that we might share in your eternal wealth. Have mercy on those whose wealth keeps them from your kingdom. Search them out and bring them salvation.

MARY MAGDALENE
A New Life

"There were many women there, looking on from a distance, who had followed Jesus from Galilee, ministering to him. Among them were Mary Magdalene, and Mary the mother of James and Joseph, and the mother of the sons of Zebedee" (Matthew 27:55-56).

ADVERTISEMENTS in Sunday newspaper supplements often cater to people searching for quick, painless solutions to vexing situations. It could be the receding hairline of middle age that bothers a man so much that he would pay $12.95 for any liquid that promises to promote the growth of fuzz on a balding scalp! "Before" and "after" pictures of women in bathing suits guarantee the same dramatic weight loss in a matter of weeks for anyone with an ounce of trust in an "amazing new diet plan."

How many churchgoers sit through Sunday sermons filled with the language of new life and spiritual transformation yet consider such language worthy of as much trust as the ads for miracle products in the Sunday magazine lying on the kitchen table after church! The Bible has its own way of giving "before" and "after" portraits that promise transformation to anyone with an ounce of faith in the God who always seems to choose those who are weak in the world's estimation to reduce to nothing those who are considered to be something, so that no human being might boast before God. The Gospel portrait of Mary Magdalene is a good example.

The Gospel is content to introduce Mary from the Galilean hamlet of Magdala simply as one "from whom seven demons had gone out" (Luke 8:2). We are left wondering what this might actually mean. The Bible does not cater to our curiosity for the scandalous secrets of famous people, especially religious personalities. In the Gospel portrait, Mary Magdalene is both weakness and strength, shame and glory, need and fulfillment. The Gospels slip quietly over her weakness, shame and need. No need to go into detail. We are all of the earth. We all have skeletons in the closet, memories of mistakes, the wounds of relationships that started like heaven but left us in pain.

The tenacity of her personal devotion to Jesus made her impervious to the dangerous situation of being clearly associated with him on Calvary. The Jewish religious leaders may not have had sophisticated intelligence gathering techniques as modern police states do, but they could make a mental note of the faces of people who would stand by the messianic pretender in his last hours when "religious" people believed it was better that one man die than that the whole nation be crushed by possible Roman reaction to popular rebellion.

This Mary who stood by the cross of Jesus would be commissioned by the risen Jesus to go to his brothers and to tell them that "I am going to my Father and your Father, to my God and your God" (John 20:17). The Bible often prefers to concentrate on the positive effects of spiritual transformation rather than the impoverished state of affairs before meeting the Lord. The Gospel invites us to follow Mary Magdalene's example, to allow Jesus to transform us from within by changing our spiritual destitution to the abundance of new life. We are challenged to remain steadfast when our faith and devotion to Jesus of Nazareth propel us into the public forum where our fidelity to Christian principles may be dismissed as hypocritical or unenlightened by the standards of the current secular mold.

Prayer

LORD, Mary Magdalene experienced change far surpassing anything she could have imagined. Have I stifled your transforming action in my life?

☆ ☆ ☆

JUDAS
Compassion and Consolation

"Then, Judas his betrayer, seeing that Jesus had been condemned, deeply regretted what he had done.... Flinging the money into the temple, he departed and went off and hanged himself" (Matthew 27:3-5).

WHO really knows what powerful forces battle in the heart of a person who commits suicide? Friends and coworkers, spouses and psychiatrists all give their postmortem suggestions. Grave financial setbacks, the prognosis of painful terminal illness, or unexpected psychotic rampages of violence emerge in newspaper accounts to explain these human tragedies. Outsiders can find a reason to a point, but there is a vast unknown world within the victim hidden to all unless an authentic message is left behind.

Judas left no suicide note. The evangelists had the responsibility for writing his obituary. Was he an avaricious man who skimmed the common purse for his own benefit? Was he a political enthusiast who lost confidence in Jesus' program for the restoration of Israel? Was he merely a pawn on God's chessboard in which there had to be a catalyst for Jesus' death, so why not Judas?

Preachers, scholars, and casual readers of the Bible have suggested these and other motives that led a close associate of Jesus, a member of the Twelve, to betray him. Jesus had chosen Judas along with Peter, James, and the others to catch the fire of his hope-filled message. Somewhere, something went wrong. We may never know what it was.

The glimpses of Judas that the Gospels give us have all been filtered through the sieve of the New Testament conviction that God brought salvation to the world through the unlikely instrument of Jesus' cross. Old Testament images and texts were used in this perspective. For the evangelists, Judas epitomized the treachery expressed by the psalmist, "The one who ate my food has raised his heel against me" (John 13:18 — Psalm 41:10). Even the two references to Judas' death in Matthew and the Acts of the Apostles show a clear relationship to the biblical idea of slanderous enemies.

The broad portrait of Judas has an uncanny and hardly coincidental similarity to the treachery and suicidal death of King David's trusted counselor Ahithophel. He had backed the unsuccessful coup led by Absalom that initially caused David to flee Jerusalem and weep in the Mount of Olives across the Kidron Valley. When the coup failed, Ahithophel went back to his home and hanged himself.

Who really knows what powerful forces battle in the heart of a person who commits suicide? I dare say, none of us! In the presence of such sad realities, we must be compassionate and merciful in our judgment. It is the survivors, the spouses, the children, relatives, and friends who go on suffering for many years, if not till their own death.

They are the people most in need of our consolation.

Prayer

L ORD, when I feel the world crashing in around me, give me the support of your love and good friends to help me get through. When I sense this same depth of suffering in others, help me to know how to reach out to them.

PAUL
Authentic Zeal

"Saul, Saul, why are you persecuting me?" (Acts 9:4).

PAUL the Apostle (Saul as he was called with his Hebrew name) was never one to run from the truth. He pursued it from his earliest years. He mastered the teachings of the elders compiled in the Pharisaic traditions. In his zeal for truth, he was ready to weed out any heretical tendencies that might attack the God-inspired doctrines he knew so well.

The Acts of the Apostles dramatizes Saul's dedication to fighting heresy by describing him on such an investigative mission to the synagogue at

Damascus on behalf of the Jerusalem authorities. Along the way, as Acts chooses to visualize this moment of conversion, the risen Jesus speaks to Saul crumpled on the ground after a flash of light. "Saul, Saul, why are you persecuting me?" (Acts 9:4).

This question seared deeply into Saul's consciousness. What could this mean? He was on an official mission to prevent some followers of Jesus the Nazorean from disrupting the community in Damascus with the claims that this executed messianic pretender was actually the Messiah for whom Saul's own spirit yearned so deeply. His intention was noble, and he was convinced of the correctness of his actions. The hardest thing God could ask of him would be to admit that he was wrong in this matter. And that is what God asked!

We can never know what happened to Saul in that moment of conversion. Was it really a "moment," or rather, a moment of insight that started a process with far-reaching effects, like a rock thrown into a placid mountain lake. After the initial splash, the rock sinks to the bottom, but the ripples spread in ever-widening circles, moving away toward each shore. Despite the blazing light and heavenly voice of the Acts account, Paul's own references to that radical change in his thinking tend to concentrate on the "effects" rather than the "how."

It is as if, once the truth of the Damascus road had sunk into Saul's mind, he could no longer look at a Christian without realizing that identification which the risen Lord had established with each of his followers. "Now you are Christ's body, and individually parts of it" (1 Corinthians 12:27), he would write two decades later to the community he had founded at Corinth. The effects of that initial insight moved in ever-widening and ever-deepening ways in his life. His life had been placid and orderly. But God had set him apart from his mother's womb and had called him through grace to experience his Son, that Paul might proclaim him to the Gentiles.

Prayer

LORD, are there presuppositions that I have which you wish to test and challenge? I think of myself as zealous for truth, noble in intention, and quite convinced that I am right. Make me ready like Saul to follow the consequences of new insights so that the narrowness of my own limited ideas may always be shattered by the breadth and depth of your wisdom.

COVENANT
LIFE
AND
LOVE

JOSHUA
Upholding Tradition

"Then Moses summoned Joshua and in the presence of all Israel said to him, 'Be brave and steadfast, for you must bring this people into the land which the Lord swore to their fathers he would give them'" (Deuteronomy 31:7).

IT is said there is a Chinese curse that reads: May you be born in a time of transition! Joshua was so cursed. He had moved comfortably in the shadow of Moses. But the spotlight suddenly turned on him. Despite the unique role of Moses in the history of the people of God, and despite his special closeness to God, he was still only a man. He could not go on forever. Everyone knew that.

But Moses was a hard act to follow. Would the people accept a relative newcomer in the leadership position? Moses had proven himself from Pharaoh's court to Sinai and through the desert years to the banks of the Jordan. Would a few words from him be enough to guarantee the allegiance of the mustered tribes as they faced what could be the most difficult part of their march to freedom?

Certain eras of history provide the catalyst that catapults ordinary people into the roles of heroes. A well-known statesman who courageously saved the eight members of his gunboat crew in wartime

JOSHUA: UPHOLDING TRADITION

was asked by journalists what it was that made him act so heroically. His answer was, "The enemy shot my boat out from under me." Joshua had been born in a time of transition and found himself on the cutting edge of a new era for God's people.

It is not easy to assume leadership of any group in the footsteps of a charismatic leader who has blazed new paths and lived in very challenging times. But as difficult as these times might have been, it is often the aftermath of great expansion that holds an essentially greater challenge. Stabilizing the ideals of the charismatic leader into an effective way of life for the whole group calls for different gifts of personality and talent. This is true in the business world, the fields of medicine and education, and certainly in church circles.

In a sense, the greatest danger for the newly emancipated Hebrews was not when they lived under the crushing oppression of Pharaoh, nor when they narrowly escaped death at the Reed Sea and in the desert wandering. The greatest danger came when they actually settled in the land of Canaan and allowed the local culture to become their standard for success in their future life there. They made peace with the gods of the land to ensure good harvests. They forgot the God who gave them food without harvests in the desert. It fell to Joshua to blow the whistle on the whole catastrophic shift toward idolatry. "As for me and my household, we will serve the Lord" (Joshua 24:15).

The difficulty of leadership in times of transition lies in the dual challenge of remaining faithful to the best of tradition while adapting creatively to the developing contemporary situations. Such adaptation is not always heartily welcomed by the multitudes, particularly if the dead leader has achieved legendary status among his followers who can now quote his once timely words without fear that he will rise from his grave to update those words in an equally prophetic way now.

Prayer

L ORD, raise up Spirit-filled leaders in your Church, and also women and men who can bring the power of these leaders into the mainstream for the benefit of the entire Christian community and the world.

RUTH
Undying Fidelity

"Wherever you go I will go, wherever you lodge I will lodge, your people shall be my people, and your God my God" (Ruth 1:16).

WHEN Jesus referred to the divisions that would arise among families because of faith in him, he mentioned strife between daughter-in-law and mother-in-law. It was the kind of proverbial example of tension that might occur then as now in any kind of discussion, especially in jokes.

Psychologists might explain this primordial form of antipathy as an inevitable consequence of the jealousy of two women who love the same man, though in quite different ways. Perhaps the fact that this phenomenon seems to be so universal accounts for the enormous popularity of the ancient tale of Ruth's love for Naomi.

This story is such a dramatic reversal of the status quo. It inspires confidence that somewhere, sometime, love can triumph over what appears to be the inevitability of conflict. Ruth's marriage is mentioned only to set the stage for the real issue. The sacred author's central interest lies in showing how the pagan Ruth finds salvation with the people of Israel because of her love for the mother of her deceased husband.

Though marriage customs of the time would have allowed Ruth to return to her father's household and all the familiar world she had known before her marriage into this Hebrew family, she opted to stay. She had thrown in her lot with them for good or ill. Her sister-in-law had the same choice but had no scruples about leaving.

Ruth, however, stayed even when Naomi approved of her going home again. While her love is a beautiful testimony worthy of imitation, that love is set within a larger context of salvation. Because of her decision to stay with Naomi she is really committing herself to the God of Israel. This commitment would gain her a place in the genealogy of Jesus.

Love that triumphs over jealousy has a way of bringing us close to God. In Ruth's case, it meant bonding herself with this woman Naomi. For us it may mean something far more simple, like giving some of our time to others even when we know that it may not be appreciated by them. Her much-quoted readiness to go wherever Naomi would lead her invites us to be ready to go where others might lead us even when it costs something of ourselves in the process.

Prayer

LORD, bless our families with peace and goodwill. Heal the deep divisions that sometimes exist and that keep your people from growing in love and joy.

SOLOMON
Wisdom without Love

"The king . . . said: 'Cut the living child in two, and give half to one woman and half to the other' " (1 Kings 3:24-25).

MANY biblical stories have an extraordinary vividness that can deeply impress the minds of young children. This is especially true when there is an element of danger or terror present. The wisdom of Solomon, David's filial successor, has become proverbial. The biblical story used to demonstrate Solomon's genius in making correct deci-

SOLOMON: WISDOM WITHOUT LOVE

sions has an edge of terror running through it as sharp as the sword with which Solomon intended to solve his dilemma of two mothers claiming the same child.

The conflict arose because the two women who lived together, and whom the Bible clearly calls harlots, gave birth to sons just a few days apart. When one child died during the night, the mother took the other woman's baby and replaced him with the body of her dead son.

In the morning, the mischievous deed was discovered. Although the infants were so young, the offended mother clearly knew how to distinguish her child from the other. If the first woman had admitted her guilt in this attempted deception, it might have ended amicably. A grieving mother can be pardoned for such a rash deed, as long as the truth of the matter is acknowledged.

But the deceiver was not about to surrender so quickly. Appeal was made to Solomon. Both women claimed the surviving child. How would Solomon decide? If the physical likeness of mother and child had been a matter of substantial help, we might have expected a judgment on these grounds alone.

However, an attentive Bible reader would surely realize that such an exercise would have been too tame for Solomon. His biblical personality profile depicts an exuberant *aficionado* of the arts and natural sciences, a stern ruler, and a lover of beautiful women. "Get me a sword," Solomon shouted over the din of the squabbling mothers. "Cut the living child in two and give half to one woman and half to the other" (1 Kings 3:24-25). The real mother said "No!" The deceiver urged the soldier on to follow the king's orders.

What a stroke of genius! The liar was betrayed by her own disdain for the child that was not hers. The real mother's love led her to make no claim for her son so long as the child could only be spared in that way. Solomon was undoubtedly astute, a quality he had inherited from his clever father. However, the Bible insists that more than mere intellectual ability was at work here. Word spread that Solomon judged with the wisdom of God himself.

Although Solomon was extolled for his wisdom and devotion to God in constructing the original Temple at Jerusalem, he was quite like us and had a shadow side as well. His justice was biased toward his own Judean tribe. He supported his sumptuous royal court and effectively maintained his building programs and military expeditions by conscripting the bodies and financial resources of the other tribes.

Solomon's career remains a striking warning for any of us who would claim divine wisdom as a personal attribute. True wisdom that reflects God's action in us will always be wedded to fidelity to God and genuine love of our brothers and sisters in God. If we claim to have wisdom without love, we are merely a resounding gong and clashing cymbals.

Prayer

*S*PIRIT *of God, guide us in the ways of love!*

HOSEA
God's Enduring Love

"I will espouse you to me forever: I will espouse you in right and in justice, in love and in mercy; I will espouse you in fidelity, and you shall know the Lord" (Hosea 2:21-22).

THE vagaries of human love have inspired poets, songwriters, and philosophers from time immemorial. Let us not forget prophets like Hosea who lived about seven hundred and fifty years before the birth of Jesus. At that time in Israel, authentic worship of Yahweh had fallen under the influence of local Canaanite fertility cults. When the people of Israel entered the Promised Land, the greatest danger they faced was not the militant resistance of the local residents, but the insidious persuasiveness of the local religious practices.

What is a farmer to do? The Hebrew sense of life affirmed the unity of all creation. The rain fertilized its spouse the earth and eventually brought forth the fruits of grain, wine, and oil. Rhythm in nature mirrored the rhythm of human love. Man and woman come together in tender embrace. "Sons are a gift from the Lord. . . . Happy the man whose quiver is filled with them" (Psalm 127:3-5). Should not Yahweh be worshiped with ritual actions that would imitate his life-giving power?

An abundance of wine and an opportunity for sexual license with the religious seal of approval guaranteed faithful attendance for the periodic festivals at hilltop shrines. Like the Canaanites before them, the new arrivals so wedded the sense of sexual polarity in nature with the revelation of God as creator that there was little difficulty in absorbing the local rites of sacred prostitution under the umbrella of Israelite faith. It was indeed a slippery road to ruin. "Their deeds do not allow them to return to their God; for the spirit of harlotry is within them, and they do not recognize the Lord" (Hosea 5:4).

It was all so logical, and so seductively reasonable. But Yahweh was not pleased with his children's logic. Where sex is involved, the tendency to rationalization is extremely strong. Destruction was the only way to purify them so that love could try again. "So I will allure her; I will lead her into the desert and speak to her heart" (Hosea 2:16).

The Israelites were on to something when they wedded their love of God to sexual experience. But they fell into the trap of thinking that sexual experience with sanctuary personnel could guarantee divine blessing for themselves, their animals, and their fields. They were not the first people nor will they be the last to confuse religious practice with magical control of God. Likewise, the tendency to divinize sexual experience as an end in itself seems an ever-present temptation. The ancient myths are never far from us, despite our boasting that we have put such childishness to rest forever.

"When Israel was a child, I loved him, out of Egypt I called my son. The more I called them, the farther they went from me" (Hosea 11:1-2). Israel had a short memory, a trait that has doomed many other peoples like them to repeat history's tragedies. Hosea dramatized the prodigality of God's forgiving love by not rejecting his prostitute wife. God has an enduring love for us even when we fail him.

Prayer

GOD of mercy and steadfast love, forgive us when we abuse your many gifts of nature and grace.

☆ ☆ ☆

JAMES AND JOHN
Worldly Ambition

"Teacher, we want you to do for us whatever we ask of you. . . . Grant that in your glory we may sit one at your right and the other at your left" (Mark 10:35-37).

THE study of history alerts us to the fact that from one generation to the next, not much is new "under the sun." This is especially true when we think of the way people with power rule over other people. Even though it was not always possible or safe for a king or queen to trust one's children to keep their subordinate place until their time to rule had come, it worked as often as not.

Modern dictatorial regimes, and even democratic governments, have also seen a certain practical wisdom in putting power only into the hands of trusted relatives or friends. Whether it was "Baby Doc" succeeding "Papa Doc" in Haiti, or the famous American Kennedy brothers in the 1960's, family ties often play a significant role in power sharing.

The Gospels do not imply that Jesus was in any way related to James and John, the fishermen sons of Zebedee. Yet those same Gospels do ascribe to them, along with Simon Peter, a special relationship of trust with Jesus in such scenes as the Transfiguration on the mountain and the agony in the garden of Gethsemane. Perhaps, then, we should not be too surprised or harsh in our judgment when we read of their request to share the top places alongside Jesus himself when he comes into his kingdom.

In Matthew's version of the incident, their mother makes the request for them. This may have been the actual way it happened or perhaps an attempt by the evangelist to salvage their halo of humility by shifting the ambitious idea to their good Jewish mother who wanted the best for her sons. And we must admit that Jewish mothers are not unique in this admirable quality!

Still, though everyone's intentions may have been far more altruistic than presently appears in the Gospels, Jesus made clear that there is no crown without the cross. And anyway, the Father in heaven would see to the distribution of awards in his good time and manner.

Once the daring request had been duly set aside, these two brothers did not back off, shut up in their own resentment. They would stick with

Jesus no matter what it might cost. Jesus even came to their defense when the other ten disciples took a dim view of their untimely request. All twelve had to learn that the Master's kingdom was not of this world. Therefore, the power sharing would not be in the earthly mold.

All of them would receive the Holy Spirit. That power would not lead to enmity between them, but to unity that no mere human disagreement could stifle. "You will receive power when the holy Spirit comes upon you, and you will be my witnesses in Jerusalem, throughout Judea and Samaria, and to the ends of the earth" (Acts 1:8).

James and John hoped for top places in the kingdom. They got far more than they requested. And momma was probably happy for them too.

Prayer

LORD, you know the powerlessness of so many people on the earth. Their cries of pain come to you without ceasing. Let your Christian people always use the power at their disposal to bring peace through justice throughout the world.

FRIENDS OF A PARALYTIC
Commitment to Jesus

"They came bringing to him a paralytic carried by four men. Unable to get near Jesus because of the crowd, they opened up the roof above him. After they had broken through, they let down the mat on which the paralytic was lying" (Mark 2:3-4).

THIS scene has a memorable quality because it shows the kind of determination that flows from strong faith. The Gospels speak of Jesus, scribes, and Pharisees all crowded together in a house at Capernaum. The friends of the paralytic were not dismayed by the crowd but took matters into their own hands. They had little difficulty breaking through the straw roof matted together with dried clay.

Jesus was a man of action as well as a teacher of religious truth. For him the lines were not so neatly drawn as they were for his scholarly interrogators. The Gospel description has comic quality as the roof progressively falls in while opponents of Jesus engage him in questions of orthodoxy. He belongs to people in need. They will not give him rest.

When the persistent friends of the paralytic had lowered their burden of love into the midst of the august assembly, the Gospels speak of the Master's admiration for their faith. He pronounced a word of forgiveness of sin, a word that sent his critics into a tantrum about Jesus usurping a privilege reserved to God alone.

The irony of this criticism is not lost on the Christian community, which finds in this story a true confession of its own faith in Jesus as Messiah. "That you may know that the Son of Man has authority to forgive sins on earth" (Mark 2:10), he heals the paralytic, almost as an afterthought. The real issue in life is not physical infirmity that afflicts our body, but spiritual weakness that obstructs our friendship with God.

The friends of the paralytic dramatize so clearly the passionate commitment of the true believer in every age. In recent decades, we have witnessed with greater frequency and success massive popular demonstrations in all corners of the world where committed believers take to the streets to manifest their solidarity with the cause of justice and peace.

We have seen tens of thousands of ordinary people confront tanks and heavily armed troops with their defenseless human bodies in order to restore sanity to societies bent on militaristic suicide. We have read accounts of massive civil protests in which ordinarily sedate grandmothers courageously link arms with college students and victims of ethnic bias in peaceful acts of civil disorder that end in imprisonment. True believers pursue their goals at great personal risk. One gets the impression from this Gospel story that Jesus would be found in their ranks today where ordinary people call for a halt to social lunacy that brings self-destruction rather than healing for the physical and spiritual wounds of the human race.

Of course, headstrong individuals can also lead whole nations into collective suicide on battlefields or into patterns of life that are totally demeaning. But, if we take Christ and his teachings for our model, we can be sure that whatever sacrifice we make for the truth will be fruitful in some way, even though we may not always accomplish our goal as the friends of the paralytic did.

Prayer

LORD, give us the faith that brooks no obstacle when it comes to helping someone in need. Inspire us in our efforts to confront tyranny in all its forms. Sustain us with the support of good friends lest we falter in our objectives.

THE POOR WIDOW
A Generous Heart

"Amen, I say to you, this poor widow put in more than all the other contributors to the treasury. For they have all contributed from their surplus wealth, but she, from her poverty, has contributed all she had, her whole livelihood" (Mark 12:43-44).

GOD is spirit, and the revelation of God's salvific love is spiritual and freely given to all people. But this revelation must be announced through the whole world by human ministers. Like any other earthbound organization, religious institutions are subject to the laws of growth and decline. Money is an essential element in the formula for growth.

Whether we think of a worldwide Christian denomination or a local synagogue, mosque, or church assembly, we know that little will happen if the collection plate does not make its rounds

POOR WIDOW: A GENEROUS HEART

regularly among the gathered faithful. The managers of the Jerusalem Temple were not exactly plagued with annual deficits like the much publicized Vatican expense account just to keep the lights on in St. Peter's. However, they knew that generous freewill offerings over and above the payment of the annual Temple tax were important for their livelihood.

Wealthy people were not usually shy about making their offerings in good sight of the pilgrims. If there had been TV news crews around in 29 A.D., they would have been called in for the handing over of the shekels. But the poor widow wouldn't have gotten much press coverage, and possibly not much acknowledgment from the officials.

Jesus was not impressed with pomp and circumstance, especially in money matters. For him, the poor widow is the real heroine in this whole matter of financial support for the Lord's earthly operations. The quality of a person's gift of self matters more than the amount of one's contribution. This applies to rich and poor alike. Every church community from the most wealthy to the poorest receives wrinkled envelopes from anonymous donors whose handwriting has been reduced to a scrawl by age and arthritis. They are the poor widows of every era, made proverbial by this woman of the Gospel who caught Jesus' attention one day as she made her offering unnoticed by the rest of the crowd.

Just as money contributes to growth, it can also too often be the cause of abuses and the reason for the ultimate decline of whole church communities. Unfortunately, the ministers of God's revelation and the various officials of their church organizations are not immune to the insidious power of money on a grand scale. Mismanagement or greed can spell disaster for the ministry of salvation.

This woman of the Gospel has gone unnamed into its pages, but she continues to shout loudly through her example to all who come to make their donation to the earthly coffers of the Lord's men and women. By her example she says, "Know that the Church has been built on the pennies of the poor, as well as the dollars of the rich. Forget not the generosity of those who have little, but who seek to share that small amount with all the generosity of their heart."

Prayer

LORD, keep me sensitive to the generosity of those who give so much when I might think of it as so little. Never let me forget your love for the poor.

THE STOOPED WOMAN
Religious Hypocrisy

"Hypocrites! Does not each one of you on the sabbath untie his ox or his ass from the manger and lead it out for watering? This daughter of Abraham whom Satan has bound for eighteen years now, ought she not to have been set free on the sabbath day from this bondage?" (Luke 13:15-16).

EIGHTEEN years is a very long time. In the lifetime of a young person, many changes occur from infancy to childhood and adolescence. For a young adult looking ahead, eighteen years still seems to be an extremely long segment of life. Even for an older person accustomed to thinking more in terms of decades than individual years, eighteen years can be a heavy burden when physical infirmity is one's daily companion.

While Jesus was teaching in a synagogue on a certain sabbath, he noticed a woman in the back of the room who was bent over. In fact, she was so completely incapable of standing erect that she often went unnoticed in crowded places. Over the years, she had learned to avoid crowds because people had little concern for anyone with a physical handicap, and she was tired of being shoved out of the way or unable to see what was going on.

She had once walked tall and jostled with all the other women at the village well. She had hoisted her plump children in her arms and carried them home from religious festivals sound asleep. But those carefree days were long gone now. In these last eighteen years, she had not known such simple joys. She had learned to look at the world from another angle. More striking than her changed perspective was the fact that the townspeople looked at her in a different way. Though her infirmity sometimes made people wonder if it were a punishment from God for some secret sin, she did not resort to such a farfetched idea.

Before and after this infirmity had developed, she had remained faithful to God. Not even her increasing debility made her curse her creator, Blessed be he! She was patient, and as so often happens in the crucible of suffering, she had become an example of sensitive concern for other people who were overlooked and outcast, even though their bodies were healthy and they should have been well accepted by other people. She had discovered that her physical infirmity did not really imprison her spirit, which rejoiced in God while so many other people were spiritually infirm despite their sleek bodies and well-groomed skin.

She did not ask anything of Jesus. He took the first step. "Woman, you are set free of your infirmity" (Luke 13:12). She looked upward at him, but then he laid his hands on her and she was able to straighten up. She glorified the God she had followed so faithfully throughout her illness.

Not all rejoiced in her sabbath day good fortune. But when the synagogue leader rebuked her, Jesus came to her rescue a second time. By his straightforward answer, Jesus showed who was really crippled and bent—anyone who would seek to truss up God's power within human expectations and religious legalism. Jesus had little tolerance for the people who equated religious custom with a personal relationship with God. The two should go together, but too often they do not. Do we find ourselves in this story?

Prayer

L ORD, free us from the spiritual infirmity of substituting religious ritual for a deep, personal relationship with you.

THE GOOD SHEPHERD
Searching for the Sheep

"What man among you having a hundred sheep and losing one of them would not leave the ninety-nine in the desert and go after the lost one until he finds it?" (Luke 15:4).

FEW of us have ever met a shepherd. In fact, if it were not for a visit to a public zoo, many urban children might never see a live sheep. Children born in biblical times, as well as those born in rural settings today, lived shoulder to shoulder with flocks of sheep and goats.

These children learned very early how to recognize the anxious bleating of lost sheep in the twilight of long summer evenings. Being young and fragile themselves, these children knew how important it was to find the lost ones before the nocturnal foxes silenced those insistent cries forever.

It seems that Jesus had shared that childhood experience because he captured so well in his parable of the lost sheep both the anxiety of being lost and the joy of rescue. Having ninety-nine sheep safely in the sheep pen for the night was good, but not good enough. Even if only one were errant, the shepherd could not nonchalantly call it a day until he had brought the unfortunate one home on his shoulders. Only then could he consider his task accomplished.

Jesus gathered just a handful of disciples initially. With the passage of centuries, the shepherds of his Church were occupied from morn till sundown just keeping the institution going from day to day. There were certainly enough people to keep a pastor close to the church building, without thinking of searching for a few "lost sheep." At the same time, "lost sheep" had the nasty habit of raising all kinds of critical problems and questions. They often implied in no uncertain terms that all was not as it should be in the Church that claimed Jesus as its founder.

Church leaders could always appeal to the astronomical numbers on their worldwide baptismal registers and the success of large-scale religious spectacles to justify their lack of attention to the wanderers from the fold. But as an insider critic of this same Church has cynically commented, "It is easier to run circuses than to look for lost sheep."

Since the Second Vatican Council, the biblical images of the Church as sheepfold, flock, vine and branches, and other New Testament images have once more come to prominence. Many pastors have enlisted the help of their capable and willing laity to go out to the lost sheep. Many Church teachers have taken up the critical questions about doctrine, worship, and moral life that formerly practicing members of the Church have asked. Many laity have responded zealously to the new emphasis on their baptismal mission to evangelize the world, beginning with their own household, family, and neighborhood.

Prayer

L ORD, may all who share your pastoral concern today search out the Christian believers who no longer find life among your Christian people. Make our sleep a bit more restless until we have begun to give attention to those who long for the Lord but cannot find the way back.

THE PRODIGAL SON
Showing Compassion

"Then let us celebrate with a feast, because this son of mine was dead, and has come to life again; he was lost, and has been found" (Luke 15:23-24).

JESUS had a keen eye for his audience. His sensitivity to the drama of life enabled him to touch the hearts of his listeners with the right dose of healing counsel. When Jesus told the story that we traditionally call "the parable of the prodigal son," he was reaching a lot of people. The human drama in that story is a staple factor of family life everywhere on planet earth and in every era of history.

Jesus spoke of a father who must silently watch as his younger son precipitously leaves home to go out into the big world. We do not hear of the father's pain. But we know it was deep, because that father never stopped looking down the road stretching from his front door to the horizon. He kept faithful vigil there, watching for the freedom boy's return. It is not hard to imagine the comments that would have made the rounds among the neighbors. "What shame that a father could not control his youngest who had no love for his family and home!" We hear such things all the time.

One day, the father's vigilance was rewarded. At first, he was not sure. After all, his eyes were not so strong anymore. But he recognized that familiar way of walking. Yes, even at a distance the father could tell that the wayward son was coming home.

The father's heart beat faster. He hurried down the road. No time for apologies now. "Bring some clothes, the ring, new shoes!" The son who was as good as dead had come back to life, back to his true home.

The father was so lavish in his forgiveness, putting past hurts behind him. Apparently, however, a forgiving spirit is not something handed on in genes. The older son who had remained at home had little compassion for his immature brother. The father's extravagant reaction to that spendthrift's homecoming only aggravated the situation.

People of compassion often seem to be too kind, too easy on those who repent only when they have fallen on hard times. There is something deep in human nature that demands punishment and feeds a vindictive spirit. Vengeance seems to be fully justified and without argument in many cases.

This father was not blessed in either of his sons. The immaturity of the younger was not necessarily more reprehensible than the narrowminded self-righteousness of the elder. Did the latter not enjoy daily the providential care of his resourceful father?

Indeed, the father may well have suffered more from the elder son's remarks than from the saddening but somewhat understandable immaturity of the younger son. The elder might have stayed around the house, but he had not grown in the loving spirit of his compassionate father. Do we find ourselves embarrassed by that elder son's failure in compassion—or do we take his side?

Prayer

LORD Jesus, you taught your disciples about the compassion of your heavenly Father not only in words but most of all in your deeds. Grant us the same spirit of compassion, especially when the surging tide of vengeance troubles our inner spirit. Remind us that we all rest in the hands of a compassionate Father.

THE DISCIPLES OF EMMAUS
Redemptive Suffering

"We were hoping that he would be the one to redeem Israel" (Luke 24:21).

THE two disciples trudging along the road from Jerusalem to Emmaus on the first Easter Sunday afternoon portray a very common situation in life. Their hopes had been raised, their enthusiasm ignited by the preaching and the deeds of Jesus of Nazareth. For whatever reason they had originally followed the crowds surrounding him, they had definitely become involved with some degree of perseverance.

They had listened to him intently, but they were not prepared for the depressing turn of events at Jerusalem. The chief priests and rulers handed Jesus over to the Romans who put an end to the hopes of many of Jesus' followers.

But along that road, they learned a most important lesson—one we all need to learn. By their very human standards and expectations, Jesus had indeed failed. What more was there to do but to go back to their roots, back to the familiar places they called home before he had come into their lives?

They had to learn to see their own world, their own precious dreams, from a new perspective. He posed the disturbing question to them, "Was it not necessary that the Messiah should suffer these things and enter into his glory?" (Luke 24:26). Their first response would have been, "No." Suffering had played no part in the scenario they had imagined.

And so it is with us too. Suffering—as inevitable as it is in everyone's life—always seems to catch us offguard. It always comes "at the wrong time," as it did for those enthusiastic disciples of Jesus.

We would never choose suffering since we see no positive value in it. But, in fact, God chose to enter into that most universal and most inevitable human experience in order to turn our perspective upside down forever.

The disciples may have lived a great many years, but on that Easter afternoon they were schoolboys again walking along with their teacher. Of course, they did not recognize him, but later they would admit that their hearts were burning within them as he spoke to them on the way and opened the scriptures to them.

In a sense, they learned their lesson without too much personal cost. We are not all so fortunate. Indeed, those Emmaus disciples seem to be almost the exception to the rule of life. Newspapers and television graphically present a parade of suffering people from morning until night. God could have redeemed us in some other way, but since we are all very much like the disciples on the road, we should be grateful that he did not leave us to figure out suffering on our own. By the suffering and death of Jesus, we have found hope even in the midst of our suffering. Death, where is your sting?

Prayer

JESUS, crucified for love of me, help me to bear the suffering that comes to my life, particularly when I suffer because of my love for you. Help me by my faith and patience to help other people for whom suffering is only a dead end street.

THOMAS
Unwavering Faith

"Jesus said to him, 'Have you come to believe because you have seen me? Blessed are those who have not seen and have believed' " (John 20:29).

WE usually remember famous people because they were present at a certain historic event, a special celebration, or even a disaster. Among the group of the disciples whom the evangelists customarily name "the Twelve," Thomas has become legendary as "doubting Thomas" precisely because he was absent when the risen Jesus appeared to that group on Easter evening.

Thomas did not hear the Master's reassuring "Peace be with you" (John 20:19). He did not see the pierced hands and side. He did not share the joy they had at seeing the Lord. He did not receive on that occasion the anointing of the Holy Spirit for the ministry of reconciliation from sin.

The Gospel according to John offers no excuse for Thomas' absence. However, his misfortune on Easter became a blessing for him and countless generations of Christian believers ever since. Thomas would not accept the word of the others that they had seen the Lord. Instead, he asked for a rerun, another appearance. He could not trust their word alone. There is a bit of Thomas in all of us. "Unless I see the mark of the nails in his hands and put my finger into the nailmarks and put my hand into his side, I will not believe" (John 20:25).

It was that simple. "Doubting" Thomas needed the undeniable factor of personal experience before he could affirm his faith in the risen Christ. The Lord obliged him by coming a week later to the same locked room. This time the doubter was not to be left out. "Put your finger here and see my hands, and bring your hand and put it into my side, and do not be unbelieving but believe" (John 20:27).

Stunned into belief, Thomas made his memorable profession, "My Lord and my God" (John 20:28). He was lucky to have had a second chance at seeing the Lord. But that is not the case for the rest of us. We are included among those whom Jesus called blessed because, though we have not seen, we believe.

Doubting Thomas had something we do not have—personal experience of the risen Jesus whom he had known before Calvary, before Easter. For us, the story of Thomas is just one more ancient witness upon which we must ultimately place our trust if we are to affirm Christian faith. Trust, pure and simple, is trust in the witness of the Twelve and the evangelists and the early Christian teachers whose writings testify to the tenacity of Christian faith in spite of dungeon, fire, and sword.

Faith is not really faith if we already see the Lord in risen splendor. When doubts arise within us, we can find some consolation in the story of Thomas. But, ultimately, we are called to that blessedness of believing without having seen, something more challenging than the call of the Twelve themselves.

Prayer

LORD, we believe though we have not seen your glory with our earthly sight. Strengthen us in time of doubt. May others find faith in you through our own perseverance.

☆ ☆ ☆

STEPHEN
Serving God's Community

"The Twelve called together the community of the disciples and said, 'It is not right for us to neglect the word of God to serve at table. Brothers, select from among you seven reputable men, filled with the Spirit and wisdom, whom we shall appoint to this task, whereas we shall devote ourselves to prayer and to the ministry of the word' " (Acts 6:2-4).

THE Second Vatican Council mandated the restoration of the permanent diaconate through which married and unmarried laymen are called to ordination for certain ministries. Diligent study of Church tradition brought about this timely and effective development. It was definitely an old idea whose time had come again.

STEPHEN: SERVING GOD'S COMMUNITY

The Acts of the Apostles portrays the origin of diaconal ministry as an innovative response to new demands that arose with the numerical growth of the Christian community. The fact that the initial need was "serving at table" should not lead us to think that deacons were, or are meant to be, simply glorified waiters! Acts gives much more attention to the evangelical ministry of that first group of seven pioneers.

Deacon Stephen's success in evangelization earned him the same mortal destiny as his Master, Jesus. False accusations led to an inquisition before the Sanhedrin. Stephen proclaims the Christian gospel by tracing a panoramic perspective stretching from Abraham to "the righteous one, whose betrayers and murderers you have become" (Acts 7:52). With a masterful touch of literary parallelism and a clear echo of the forgiving love of the crucified Jesus, Stephen cries out while boulders pummel him to death, "Lord Jesus, receive my spirit.... Do not hold this sin against them" (Acts 7:59-60).

Deacon Philip stars in a most significant scene of Christian conversion. The Spirit of God led Philip to the side of an Ethiopian court official traveling home from worship at Jerusalem. When Philip heard the man read about a sheep led to the slaughter in the servant song of Isaiah 53, he asked the official, "Do you understand what you are reading?" The man's answer exquisitely portrays the real challenge of biblical study and religious education. "How can I, unless someone instructs me?" (Acts 8:30-31).

Philip wasted no time in seizing this prime occasion for evangelization. He started on the wavelength of his questioner and made sense of what formerly left the inquirer confused. Philip's attentiveness and faith-filled counseling led to the official's conversion and baptism.

Men called to diaconal ministry in today's Church can find in the New Testament accounts of their predecessors a mandate to announce the Christian gospel in word and deed. The ordination ceremony dramatically represents their primary mission to evangelize along with the related responsibilities as ministers of sacraments and worship. In addition, they assist the Church in secular matters in which they enjoy some competence.

Filled with the Spirit and wisdom, these men continue in the steps of Stephen and Philip, whose service was never limited to matters of community management. These modern deacons give understanding to those who need instruction and bread to those who are hungry.

Prayer

LORD, raise up in your Church good and faithful leaders to serve as deacons on behalf of your people. Give them your Spirit and the wisdom that comes from above.

LYDIA
Apostolic Women

"On the sabbath, we went outside the city gate along the river where we thought there would be a place of prayer. We sat and spoke with the women who had gathered there" (Acts 16:13).

TOO many otherwise highly educated people still have the distorted impression that Paul the Apostle was a misogynist, or at least that he wanted all teaching authority and Church administration firmly centered in male leadership. Popular novelists and fundamentalist approaches to writings attributed to Paul have fostered these mistaken ideas. Pauline scholars today readily make a distinction between Paul's own letters and the pastoral collection of First and Second Timothy and Titus most likely penned by his disciples some decades after his death.

When Paul is allowed to stand alone, his letters clearly show his endorsement of equality for men and women in every Church matter upon which he explicitly comments. He recognized how men and women marvelously enrich the Body of Christ with the diversity of their personal gifts.

The Acts of the Apostles depicts a man genuinely open in social rapport and Church ministry with all sorts of people. On Paul's initial arrival at Philippi, a prominent Roman colony in Northeastern Greece around 50 A.D., the heart of Lydia, a Greek businesswoman, was opened to Paul's preaching. Her whole household accepted baptism, and then she made Paul an offer he could not refuse. "If you consider me a believer in the

Lord, come and stay at my home" (Acts 16:15). Like so many other women throughout history, she got her way.

The impact of Lydia and the other converts at Philippi upon Paul has been immortalized in Paul's own letter to this community several years later. "I give thanks to my God at every remembrance of you, praying always with joy in my every prayer for all of you, because of your partnership for the gospel from the first day until now.... I hold you in my heart, you who are all partners with me in grace, both in my imprisonment and in the defense and confirmation of the gospel. For God is my witness, how I long for all of you with the affection of Christ Jesus" (Philippians 1:3-8).

Should we not think of Lydia in the first instance, since Paul made her home his base of operation? Her generosity to Paul was the outcome of her faith in Christ. Humanly speaking, Lydia and Paul may have had little in common, but the Christ they did share bound them together in a way that no human prejudice could ever subvert. "There is neither Jew nor Greek, there is neither slave nor free person, there is not male and female; for you are all one in Christ Jesus" (Galatians 3:28).

Paul's association with Lydia and the Church community that began to meet at her home gives us an inspiring example of the way Christian fellowship grew within local communities and across great distances through the journeys of the missionaries crisscrossing the great highways of the Roman Empire. Paul was open to every person who was ready to meet the risen Christ. Paul rejoiced in the ministry he shared with men and women alike. In our own day, that clear image of Christian apostolic action by men and women together is a reminder that every member of the Body of Christ is called to evangelize the world.

Prayer

LORD, stir up your Christian people that they will take up their rightful place in preaching the Gospel to all nations, beginning with their own household and neighborhood.

PRISCA AND AQUILA
Dedicated Laity

"Greet Prisca and Aquila, my co-workers in Christ Jesus, who risked their necks for my life, to whom not only I am grateful but also all the churches of the Gentiles; greet also the church at their house" (Romans 16:3-5).

SEVERAL husband and wife teams are well known in the entertainment world. Likewise, in political circles, many wives are often perceived to be the brains behind their duly elected President-husbands! Because Roman Catholic Church leadership has been so consistently vested in celibate priests, we have not been accustomed to thinking of husband and wife teams in church ministry.

Yet, back in the beginning, slipped in between the exploits of Paul the Apostle, we discover

Aquila and Prisca (or Priscilla as she is called in the Acts of the Apostles), ministering to Paul, to the Alexandrian scripture scholar Apollos, and to the community at Ephesus that gathered in their home for worship.

It appears that Aquila and Prisca originally lived in Rome as members of the Jewish community at the heart of the Roman Empire. When disturbances in the synagogue community around the year 49 A.D. apparently caught the ear of Emperor Claudius who had little tolerance for Jewish quarrels just outside his bedroom window on the Palatine Hill, he ordered an expulsion of some or a great number of the community from Rome itself. Apparently, Aquila and his wife migrated to Corinth, where Paul stayed with them when he arrived there around 50 A.D. He was not a burden to them but worked alongside them in the tent-making trade.

Although the local hard-line Jews tried to get Paul into trouble with the Roman magistrate, they were not successful in having the Roman proconsul remove Paul from the scene since that clever foreigner had learned to keep away from religious feuds. However, the handwriting was on the wall, so after a while Paul, Aquila, and Prisca moved on together. Paul went on to Syria, but Aquila and his wife set up home at Ephesus.

Here the scriptures speak of them ministering to Apollos who needed an update course in Christianity, despite his brilliance in biblical exegesis in the Alexandrian tradition. The Church was more than the scriptures. After some assistance from Prisca and Aquila, his ministry took on more clarity and power.

This couple made a striking contribution to the early Church. Although the apostolic labors of the laity have often been overlooked in the writings of church history, there have been hundreds of thousands of people like Prisca and her husband who have evangelized their neighborhoods, carried the gospel to foreign lands, and generously welcomed other church ministers into the privacy of their own home.

The extraordinary example of faith in action given by Prisca and Aquila is constantly repeated in the zeal of many modern couples, particularly in movements such as Catholic Family Movement, Cursillo, Marriage Encounter, and Catholic Charismatic Renewal. Every baptized person is called to holiness and to share in the missionary apostolate of the Church. This ideal is now coming to realization with each passing day.

Prayer

LORD, raise up among us strong Catholic couples who will witness to your transforming grace in their married lives. May their experience of community deepen the community of faith that we share in Christ Jesus, your Son.

ANNOUNCING
THE
GOOD
NEWS

JESUS OF NAZARETH
Bearer of Good News

"Jesus returned to Galilee in the power of the Spirit, and news of him spread throughout the whole region. He taught in their synagogues and was praised by all. He came to Nazareth, where he had grown up, and went according to his custom into the synagogue on the sabbath day" (Luke 4:14-16).

IT started as just another familiar sabbath service. There was the usual order of the singing of psalms and the intercessory prayers. The walls of the little building echoed once again with the ancient reminder to the assembly that they should "hear, O Israel! The Lord is our God, the Lord alone! Therefore, you shall love the Lord, your God, with all your heart, and with all your soul, and with all your strength" (Deuteronomy 6:4-5).

After the selected reading from the Torah, Jesus was given the scroll of Isaiah the prophet. He unrolled it and began to read. "The Spirit of the Lord is upon me, because he has anointed me to bring glad tidings to the poor. He has sent me to proclaim liberty to captives and recovery of sight to the blind, to let the oppressed go free, and to proclaim a year acceptable to the Lord" (Luke 4:18-19).

The whole scene unfolds with a solemnity characteristic of religious ceremonies in many diverse cultures. Religious worship taps deeply into a person's self-identity. Hearing the prayers familiar from one's youth brings reassurance as the twilight years exact their progressive toll on the human body and spirit. In the midst of all life's challenges, religious prayers, symbolic rituals and sacred scriptures provide a bulwark against the changes that can disturb us.

Since so much of the regular service was a collection of formal prayers and ancient readings, most faithful worshipers did not come to synagogue with any expectation of revolutionary events. Revolution was what the Zealot political party was constantly plotting against the Roman military presence in this volatile Galilean territory. Revolution was a dream in the hearts of slaves whose spirits were crushed by the paternalistic manipulation that made them cogs in an economic system elaborately sanctioned to enrich the power class. Revolutions did not begin in synagogues on sleepy sabbath mornings—at least not until today.

No one expected revolutionary words from Jesus, the son of Joseph and Mary. When he sat down to give the traditional sermon for the day, he caught them unprepared for the momentous announcement he summed up in one short sentence. "Today this scripture passage is fulfilled in your hearing" (Luke 4:21).

The congregation's admiration for his comments was etched with a bit of wonderment since they knew his family. It is a strange human foible that we often give more weight to the words of foreigners than we do to our hometown men and women. The initial good feeling toward Jesus changed dramatically when he recalled the scriptural stories of Elijah and Elisha, hometown men who had been rejected by Israel. Through their ministry to the woman of Zarephath and Naaman the Syrian, Gentile "outsiders," God showed his love for all people.

As so often happens with crowds of disgruntled people, the mood of the assembly reached a fever pitch of resentment. The evangelist even tells us they intended to hurl Jesus over a cliff. "But he passed through the midst of them and went away" (Luke 4:30).

This story clearly proclaims the unique mission Jesus had to announce the good news of salvation of which the Hebrew scriptures had spoken for centuries. The people were not bothered by the words of Isaiah, but by the way in which Jesus identified himself with this mission. Their shock at his words on this sabbath would grow throughout the coming years as he spelled out more concretely in words and deeds what the "good news of salvation" meant for his own day and for ours.

It was fitting that Jesus announce his mission on a sabbath since there would be many future sabbaths when he would dramatize that the Creator who had rested on the seventh day would not be constrained by the religious customs when his people were in need. Healing, exorcism, announcing the gospel to the poor—no sabbath rules could tie the hands of the God who wished to strengthen and liberate his people through Jesus of Nazareth, the son of God.

As powerful as this scene is, the Gospels always hold more secrets for us than a simple superficial reading brings to light. We must recall that all four evangelists were more interested in the lasting significance of the life, death and resurrection of Jesus than they were in merely transcribing verbatim reports of his daily activities. More attention to the creative work of Luke, the evangelist, alerts us to the truly revolutionary quality of the ministry of Jesus that is launched in the setting of the synagogue service at Nazareth.

The passage of Isaiah that Jesus reads in this scene is actually a selection of several texts carefully integrated into this "word of Jesus." The result is that the words of Isaiah have been broadened to embrace a mission of salvation toward all people rather than simply the people of Israel. The examples of Elijah and Elisha that Jesus proposes bring out this universal dimension of his own mission. Likewise, the mention of freeing "the oppressed" clearly shows that authentic evangelization must include social justice as an essential element rather than as optional icing on the cake of spiritual doctrine.

Modern Christian congregations who hear this Gospel story are often no different from the people in the Nazareth audience who were unprepared for the evangelical revolution that Jesus started. "Today" is the day of salvation. From the beginning of his ministry till the end on Calvary, Jesus would keep saying it unmistakably. "Today salvation has come to this house because this man too is a descendant of Abraham" (Luke 19:9). Even on Calvary, the mission would go forward. "Amen, I say to you, today you will be with me in Paradise" (Luke 23:43).

Do we hear the word of God with the expectation that a revolution of love and healing could change the world? Jesus invites us, no, he insists that we join together with him in the power of his Spirit to allow that revolution to shape our personal future, the future of our Church, and the future of the whole world.

Prayer

GOD of Israel, Father of our Lord Jesus Christ, stir up the hearts of your faithful people with a renewed spirit of evangelical love. Make us more sensitive to the cry of the poor that rises from every country on our planet. Help us to make "today" a time of salvation, a new experience of the freedom that is your will for us.

QOHELETH
The Perplexity of Life

"Vanity of vanities, says Qoheleth, vanity of vanities. All things are vanity!" (Ecclesiastes 1:2).

VANITY has become an old-fashioned word. The sonorous cadences of this familiar theme of the Book of Ecclesiastes have a medieval ring to them. They are not likely to grab the attention of a twentieth-century teenager. Yet the message of Ecclesiastes is so contemporary. Indeed, among all of the writings of ancient biblical literature, Ecclesiastes echoes so well the exasperation of many thinking people today.

The opening phrase that becomes a recurrent chant throughout the entire treatise expresses the author's consternation when he realizes that life is a baffling puzzle. Daily experiences confront thoughtful people with so many unanswered questions. For too many people, life remains a problem to be solved, whereas the author of Ecclesiastes suggests it is a mystery to be experienced just as it is.

Ecclesiastes, or Qoheleth, is a fictional preacher-king of Jerusalem who soliloquizes about the enigma that life presents. With all the enthusiasm of a modern fitness freak, Qoheleth pursues learning, sensual delights, and immortality in earthly terms. Despite his fanatical indulgence, he always ends up with the same conclusion. No experience of life really guarantees the kind of fulfillment for which he so diligently searches.

Besides his dissatisfaction with these many good things, Qoheleth finds particularly distressing the oppression and inhumanity that characterizes so much of what is called politics. "From the hand of their oppressors comes violence, and there is none to comfort them! And those now dead, I declared more fortunate in death than are the living to be still alive. And better off than both is the yet unborn, who has not seen the wicked work that is done under the sun" (Ecclesiastes 4:1-3).

Life is not fair. The just are treated as though they had done evil, while wicked people prosper without judgment. Certainly, journalists can find a goldmine of contemporary headlines in this provocative *tour de force* on the frustrating paradoxes of contemporary existence.

Some years ago, a famous rock group popularized the eloquent poem about time that holds a central place in Qoheleth's treatise. "There is . . . a time to be born, and a time to die . . . a time to tear down, and a time to build . . . a time to love, and a time to hate . . . a time of war, and a time of peace" (Ecclesiastes 3:2, 3, 8). In the ancient author's mind, this cycle of life's events and emotions only dramatizes human slavery to time. Yet God has placed the hunger for the timeless in our hearts with the result that we long for something beyond the present world "without . . . ever discovering from beginning to end, the work which God has done" (Ecclesiastes 3:11).

Qoheleth's vision of life was limited to the present world alone. But as St. Paul the Apostle would say, this world is passing away. Qoheleth eloquently voices the quandary of our earthbound existence. The Christian gospel enables the modern believer to face the perplexity of life with courage and inner peace.

Prayer

LORD, in the mystery of life, be my guiding light. Make my steps pure and my direction straight. Let your strength be mine, your wisdom my daily help.

☆ ☆ ☆

RAHAB
Faith Commitment

"Abraham became the father of Isaac . . . Salmon the father of Boaz, whose mother was Rahab. Boaz became the father of Obed, whose mother was Ruth" (Matthew 1:2-5).

ONLY a few women have been memorialized in the Hebrew Bible and the Christian New Testament. We stumble across references to them almost by accident, since they are seldom given the same attention as the men who fathered the tribes of Israel and acted as God's intermediaries in key moments of God's self-revelation. We hear of the song of Miriam by the Red Sea, the military exploits of Deborah, the providential courage of Judith, and Ruth's steadfast love for Naomi. But the great women of the Bible seem to be few and far between.

Anyone familiar with the paternity lists in Genesis, Chronicles, and Ezra immediately recognizes something revolutionary when Matthew includes Tamar, Rahab, Ruth, and the wife of Uriah, whose name was Bathsheba, among the ancestry of Jesus the Messiah. The story of Rahab piques the curiosity of many people because of the scandalous overtones attached to the biblical references to her as "Rahab the harlot."

Chapter 2 of Joshua records that she befriended the two Hebrew spies sent to reconnoiter the walled city of Jericho. She was a "fifth column" within the walls who cooperated with the enemy for something in return. She did not seek a gift of jewelry or some other selfish trinket. "Now then, swear to me by the Lord that, since I am showing kindness to you, you in turn will show kindness to my family" (Joshua 2:12).

The spies gave her a scarlet cord that she was to tie to the window through which they escaped from the barricaded city. How many poor women are forced to barter with their own body for some small form of economic security in cultures where destitution is the gross national product and the only easily marketable item is a person's sexual company. Rahab was spared that travesty when those two Hebrews scurried into her inn hoping to get lost in the crowd for a night lest the local militia spot them and bring their young lives to a dead halt.

Scholars point out that "harlot" may be more pejorative than the original meaning of the Hebrew word, which could simply mean a "female innkeeper." The story itself refers to the spies as house guests and offers no sexual grist for the scandal-sheet journalists who like to titillate their reading public. Indeed, her request for kindness to her extended family shows a stability of life we do not often associate with prostitution. Matthew's mention of her implies a very upright marriage relationship between Rahab and Salmon that led to the birth of Boaz, the great-grandfather of David.

Whatever the exact nature of her employment, the Bible insists that Rahab opted for allegiance to the God of Israel at great personal risk in a militarized city alive with fear of impending disaster and rumor-mongering neighbors ready to take advantage of the climate of public disorder to settle old grudges. The "scarlet cord" that gave rise to the bawdy "red light" districts of modern world capitals was once a beacon of salvation for Rahab and her family. Its modern day counterpart fosters psychosexual immaturity in individuals, wreaks havoc in families, and contributes to the spread of contagious, and even fatal, sexual diseases.

Prayer

L ORD, assist those who cry out to you in the midst of their poverty. Protect them from all harm.

AMOS
Love for the Poor

"Days are coming, says the Lord God, when I will send a famine upon the land: not a famine of bread, or thirst for water, but for hearing the word of the Lord" (Amos 8:11).

CRITICISM is hard to take even when it comes from a friend who clearly has our best interests at heart. However, most of us are a bit less open to unflattering remarks when they come from a stranger. We are more likely to question the critic's credentials and more ready to discount or deny the objective truth that provoked the comments in the first place.

We might even be anxious to get rid of this person who troubles us with the disturbing fact that all is not so perfect as we would like to pretend, but as good Pope John XXIII so often said, we should respect the truth wherever it is found. Despite all our ingenious lies and our penchant for subterfuge, truth has a way of coming to light eventually.

Amos, the shepherd of Tekoa near Jerusalem, spoke the truth fearlessly, despite the fact that his mission led him to unfriendly territory in the Northern Kingdom of Israel. It did not take long for Amaziah, the local priest in charge of the shrine at Bethel, to realize that this stranger from the other side of the border could only spell trouble for the local worshipers.

After all, there was peace and prosperity, thanks to the long reign of King Jeroboam. Property values were up. The upper classes could afford to decorate their summer houses with fine imported ivory. This year's wine would be plentiful and bring a good price. It would also keep the lower classes in a half-stupor to drown their complaints about exorbitant farm taxes and the rest of their gripes.

The last thing Bethel needed now was a loudmouth upstart from Judah talking about systematic oppression of the poor. He had also hit too close to home when he implied—no, emphatically declared—that God hates the shrine festivals and prefers justice to sacred music and sacrificial offerings.

There were always people who would justify their mediocrity in religious observance by downplaying its importance for God, but enough was enough! "Off with you, visionary, flee to the land of Judah! There earn your bread by prophesying, but never again prophesy in Bethel; for it is the king's sanctuary and a royal temple" (Amos 7:12-13).

Evening came. The gates were barred. The night air was quiet, except for the occasional cry of a rooster. But Amaziah could not sleep. The shepherd's remarks as he was being hustled out of the shrine by two assistants kept coming to mind. "Your wife shall be made a harlot in the city, and your sons and daughters shall fall by the sword; your land shall be divided by measuring line, and you yourself shall die in an unclean land; Israel shall be exiled far from its land" (Amos 7:17). Amaziah could not decide if these were just the angry threats of an unwelcome foreigner or a privileged glimpse of the future which still seemed so unlikely. "Well, time will tell. It certainly will not be settled tonight," he said as he drifted off into sleep.

Prayer

L ORD God, raise up your prophets again in our own day. Let justice roll down like a waterfall so that every land will be bathed in its healing power.

☆   ☆   ☆

ISAIAH
Peace with Justice

"For a child is born to us, a son is given us; upon his shoulder dominion rests. They name him Wonder-Counselor, God-Hero, Father-Forever, Prince of Peace" (Isaiah 9:5).

IF you were to ask a sample group of ten people their first impression of an Old Testament prophet, many of them, if not most, would describe a bearded, poorly-clad, half-crazed man shouting statements of doom in the middle of the street. But this description is more appropriate for some of the homeless and mentally ill people who wander through all the cities of the modern world than it is for the great biblical prophets of ancient Israel.

Isaiah certainly does not fit that mold. He was a man familiar with the upper class of Jerusalem society. He was at home in the corridors of power. Although he lived through some difficult decades of international intrigue and smoldering aggression on many sides, it would be naive and misleading to portray him in the colors of "doom and gloom."

Ahaz, a boy-king only twenty years of age, inherited the throne of Judah just when his northern neighbors were flexing their muscles in the face of Assyria, which had a particular flare for atrocities against its enemies. Ahaz was in a difficult bind. Should he join Samaria and Damascus in their campaign against the superpower in the north, or should he cast himself at the feet of Tiglath-pileser and give in before it was too late? Or should he listen to Isaiah, a man old enough to be his father, who came with a message from God all bound up with the promise of a child to be named Immanuel, a name that means "God-with-us"?

Perhaps if Ahaz were not king, it would have been easier for him to find comfort in the way Isaiah dismissed Syria and Israel as smoldering stumps of wood. Isaiah even claimed that Assyria would be no threat to the future of Judah! But young Ahaz could not take the chance of mixing faith with politics, so he turned a deaf ear to Isaiah's advice and called in Assyria, making sure to reinforce his pledge of allegiance with silver and gold from the Temple treasury. The rest of the story is not hard to imagine since Assyria was happy to devastate Syria and Israel without fear of reprisal from the southern border.

Of course, we will never know how different history might have been if Ahaz had followed Isaiah's advice and just played it cool, trusting in God to protect Judah. Those who wish to drive a wedge between faith and politics for the theoretical advantage of keeping politics free of religious influence may discover that they have only succeeded in creating a political monster that does not feel constrained by any religious principles. Politics does not exist in theory but in real people. And real people have a need and a tendency to be religious— whether or not they go to church or declare themselves so in a formal way.

Isaiah's encouraging promise of a wisdom-child who would shepherd God's people and rule them peacefully was partially fulfilled in his own lifetime with the birth of Hezekiah. But, more importantly for us, that child Immanuel was Jesus of Nazareth, son of David and Prince of Peace. Faith and politics were troublesome in his day as well. He would proclaim a kingdom of justice and die on the cross as a criminal.

Prayer

GRANT peace, O Lord, in our day! Send your wisdom and love.

JEREMIAH
Preaching the Word of God

"All the day I am an object of laughter; everyone mocks me.... I say to myself, I will not mention him. I will speak in his name no more. But then it becomes like fire burning in my heart, imprisoned in my bones; I grow weary holding it in. I cannot endure it" (Jeremiah 20:7, 9).

THE prophet Jeremiah lived through an explosive period of Jewish history, the last four decades before the conquest of Jerusalem by Babylonian armed forces in 598 B.C. He witnessed the subsequent deportation of the upper classes that have marked Judaism with a distinctive diaspora mentality now reinforced by the mid-twentieth-century Holocaust of Europe.

Jeremiah agonized about the idiotic rebelliousness of Judah's last kings, some of them sons of the revered Josiah who had enthusiastically pursued religious reform dear to the heart of Jeremiah. Josiah's untimely death in a misguided military action cut short the authentic renewal of heart among the citizens of Judah long before it could have borne lasting fruit in a new generation of believers.

More than all the other prophets, Jeremiah lets us look into his mind to see the steadfastness with which he lived out his prophetic ministry. "Lived out" is the operative factor in the lengthy pages of biographical and autobiographical accounts of this passionate man that his disciples and his secretary Baruch have transmitted to us.

Jeremiah's message contains oracles of judgment and salvation like the other great prophets of the previous century. However, Jeremiah's mode of presentation reveals a much more personalized union between the word of God and his own inimitable way of being himself. His commitment to the Lord was not a sabbath-type of allegiance. The word of the Lord pervaded his whole life.

Despite his initial reluctance to speak on the Lord's behalf, so forcefully dramatized in his excuse that he was too young, Jeremiah plunged into his mission with all of his native zeal. It did not involve a great journey like that of Jonah. God did not ask him to name children with prophetic symbolism like those of Hosea and Isaiah. Rather, Jeremiah's celibacy was to be a dramatic witness to the fact that the children born to parents of his generation would face death in a short time. "I will silence the cry of joy, the cry of gladness, the voice of the bridegroom and the voice of the bride" (Jeremiah 7:34).

No one likes to bring bad news, because the recipients often take out their disappointment and anger on the innocent messenger. Jeremiah protested to God about the derision that his mission evoked. "You duped me, O Lord, and I let myself be duped; you were too strong for me, and you triumphed" (Jeremiah 20:7).

Jeremiah's anguish at being a counter-cultural symbol for his own generation finds an echo today in the hearts of Christians of every socioeconomic level and ethnic background. Baptism into Christ plunges the Christian into the prophetic ministry of people like Jeremiah and Jesus. Modern Christians are derided for retaining traditional mores in sexual ethics, or for attempting to dismantle systematic economic practices that guarantee that the poor will become poorer. Like Jeremiah before them, modern Christian prophets cannot silence the Lord's word that is within them. Their bones are weary with holding it in.

Prayer

L ORD, raise up prophets in our midst whose lives will dramatically speak your living word with every fibre of their being.

SUSANNA
Perseverance in Virtue

"It is better for me to fall into your power without guilt than to sin before the Lord" (Daniel 13:23).

IN traditional stories of the good guys and the bad guys, we expect truth and justice to triumph. The story of Susanna in the appendix to the Book of Daniel has all the elements of such a struggle between a defenseless woman's innocence and the lust-inspired accusations of certain respected members of the power class.

The parade of characters reads like a TV sitcom. The modest, beautiful Susanna is the pious wife of Hilkiah, a wealthy man who lived in comfortable surroundings and whose house was frequented by the upper echelon of Jewish society in Babylon. The two "elders" were not necessarily hobbling around on canes. They are portrayed as quite astute in their attempts to satisfy their sensual curiosity, even to the point of vigorously bidding each other good-bye at lunchtime only to stumble into each other moments later furtively backtracking in the hope of catching a look at the lady of the house during her midday visit to the outdoor hot tub.

Believing that two heads were better than one, the two men made a pact to satisfy their lust by entrapping the maiden with the threat of false testimony if she would not comply with their demands. When she did not give in, but affirmed her fidelity to God, and thus to her husband as well, they had to go through with their plan. Though proverbially "hell hath no fury like the wrath of a scorned woman," it would seem the same could be said of the male of the species!

With great pomp and self-righteousness, these two elders placed their hands on her head as they gave their false testimony before the court and the people. The same hands that had sought to caress her now seek to destroy what they cannot possess. Not even Susanna's cry to God seems to move them to repentance. They would have been successful if God had not intervened through Daniel who stopped them dead in their march to victory by proving that two heads may be more dangerous than one.

When Daniel interrogated the accusers separately, they perjured themselves because they had not worked out their story well enough. One said the woman sinned with a young lover under a mastic tree, while the other claimed it was an oak. Catch the irony of these two eagle-eyed judges who never missed a pretty face on the street but could not tell the difference between a small bush and a mammoth tree. Innocent blood was spared that day. The whole assembly blessed God who saves those who hope in him.

Unfortunately, these biblical stories do not always play out in life with the same happy endings. Innocence does not always find vindication through God-inspired defenders like Daniel. Socially prestigious people do get their way very often at the expense of someone else's virtue. Power people seldom lose when they have their day in court. Despite this, Susanna's perseverance in virtue remains the best road to follow. Imprisoned prophets and lovers of truth down through the centuries have dramatized the fact that ruthless people may rob me of my life, but only I can give them my soul.

Prayer

L ORD, hear the cry of innocent victims echoing across the hills and valleys, the deserts and seas of this planet. Raise up prophets who will vindicate those who are persecuted for the sake of righteousness.

SECOND ISAIAH
Proclaiming the Good News

"A voice cries out: In the desert, prepare the way of the Lord! Make straight in the wasteland a highway for our God!" (Isaiah 40:3).

DESERTS are very dangerous places. The sun scorches every living thing by day. Water is scarce. Hardly a nourishing plant can grow. Only madmen would go into the desert on purpose. Only madmen, or men and women searching for God.

Once, the desert of Sinai had been a passageway to freedom for the Hebrew slaves in Egypt. When Moses came to lead them out, they did not think of the dangers but only of the goal. Their trust in God gave them courage for the journey. They were not disappointed.

But people can be fickle and forgetful, even of having been saved from death. It happened that the descendants of those liberated slaves, who once survived the terrors of the desert, fell prey to the bewitching delights of apostasy in their new-found freedom. They forgot the Lord who saved them. So, God hid his face from them and gave them up to the power of their sins.

Once again in bondage, now in Babylon, they heard a new Moses speak of the desert again. The prophet's name did not matter. It was really God sounding the reveille loud enough to awaken those who had grown deaf during the fifty years by the waters of Babylon.

Once again came the call to go forth. But this time, there was a difference. Babylon was not Egypt. The exile had begun with the fearful wrenching away from the homeland. However, Babylon turned out to be a blessing for the deportees from the Judean backwater beyond the Euphrates. There was no glut on the job market and the upper-crust Judeans quickly entered the mainstream of Babylonian commerce. Job security and the upwardly mobile climate definitely threw cold water on the call to return to the distant and underdeveloped hills of Judah.

The anonymous prophet of the new exodus (known as Second Isaiah) did not find a receptive audience. Many heard him but left him alone to rhapsodize as if he were a befuddled old man who had lost touch with reality. After all, the world had moved on. The patched wasteland of the Jordan Valley did not bear comparison with the sparkling waters of the Chebar and the elegant canals of Babylon itself.

"How beautiful upon the mountains are the feet of him who brings glad tidings, announcing peace, bearing good news, announcing salvation, and saying to Zion, 'Your God is King!' " (Isaiah 52:7). Prophets are amazingly resilient to lack of popular approval. When you have heard the voice of God, you learn not to measure success by box office statistics of supporters.

Evangelization has never been easy. The "good news" that we bring does not always capture the interest of those to whom we speak. Even Jesus knew such difficulties when his word went unheeded, like seed that falls on rocky ground, or like sprouting plants that are choked by thorns. But true prophets go on sounding the call from the desert to the mountaintops. And where there are people who embrace that word with a generous and good heart, they will bear fruit through perseverance.

Prayer

LORD, give us perseverance in announcing your word. Strengthen us with your spirit in the midst of an unbelieving generation.

JOHN THE BAPTIST
Bearing Witness

"The law and the prophets lasted until John; but from then on the kingdom of God is proclaimed, and everyone who enters does so with violence" (Luke 16:16).

PROPHETS have the knack of disturbing guilty consciences. They seem to have iron wills that do not allow them to flinch from their mission even in the face of threats to their bodily welfare. Prophets are ready to take the consequences for confronting power structures with the truth of their abusiveness and denigration of human beings who have no voice to speak for their own destiny.

John the Baptist strides across the early pages of the Gospels with the self-confidence of a man who has God on his side. He is a "voice in the wilderness" daring to say what others only whisper in secret. He did not fear the loneliness of his mission. He was bold and told it "like it was." King Herod had committed adultery by taking his brother's wife. People who blow the whistle on adulterous kings and other modern despots do not usually die peacefully in their beds at a ripe old age. John the Baptist was no exception to this rule.

The Gospels portray him first of all as the herald of glad tidings, the envoy dressed in the clothing of Elijah so as to be recognized unmistakably as one with a mission from God. Once, God had saved his people from the exile in Babylon, preparing in the wilderness of Arabia a superhighway of safety for their return to Jerusalem. Now God would fulfill those deeper desires for salvation from sin and death, the double trouble that haunts every man, woman, and child on planet earth.

Creative preacher that he was, John adapted his message to his specific audience. He told the tax collectors to stop filling their own pockets at the expense of their Jewish brothers and sisters by collecting more than what was prescribed by the Roman occupation government. To the soldiers who came to listen, he said, "Do not practice extortion, do not falsely accuse anyone, and be satisfied with your wages" (Luke 3:14). And to everyone without exception he said, "Whoever has two cloaks should share with the person who has none. And whoever has food should do likewise" (Luke 3:11).

Tyrants can tolerate preachers as long as the oppressor perceives their religious message to be an opium for the masses, pacifying any social consciousness that might fire them to build a new world free from all forms of oppression of body, mind, and spirit. But John's accusation of adultery was the last straw to what had become a particularly disturbing popularity campaign surrounding this desert preacher. The Gospels suggest that Herod would have been content to remove John from the public forum through incarceration.

However, in keeping with the proverbial anger of a scorned woman, Herodias used her seductive daughter to reap her own personal vindictiveness. John's head on a platter was the dancing girl's reward.

The preacher was dead, but the truth he announced could not be stopped. It took flesh again in Jesus of Nazareth and when word about Jesus reached Herod he said, "It is John whom I beheaded. He has been raised up" (Mark 6:16). Herod was both right and wrong at the same time because true prophets never die as long as their message takes flesh in the heart of another person.

Prayer

L ORD, raise up prophets of truth in our day. Give them courage in the face of danger and your comfort in their lonely journey.

THE WIDOW OF NAIN
Life out of Death

"As Jesus drew near to the gate of the city, a man who had died was being carried out, the only son of his mother, and she was a widow" (Luke 7:12).

DEATH is a cruel taskmaster. It has no mercy. It respects neither wealth nor human desires. Death cuts down the young and the old, the foolish and the intelligent, the prosperous landowner and the impoverished child of the desert sands. At times, the tragic circumstances of a particular death add a certain tone of viciousness to this silent, mysterious visitor against whom no one of us can ever be absolutely secure.

This woman of Nain had known death more than once. She had mourned with friends many a time when illness had reaped its harvest of pain and dying gasps from loved ones. She had known death when it came close to home, robbing her of the lover of her youth, the man who had stirred her heart with the deep reassurance that life could be joy-filled even in the midst of poverty.

Her sadness was great on that day, and that kind of sadness never really goes away. However, one learns to cope with life. Death offers us no alternative. Having a son to lean upon enabled her to sleep more peacefully at night. Though she had always been the one to nurture him, and even spoil him as mothers do, the time had arrived when she would need his support.

But death has no logic. Death visited her home once again. The only child, the son of promise, was gone. Perhaps if she had hidden the boy, death would never have found him. The moment of death inspires such foolish thoughts in us. Another day of grief, another funeral cortege hurrying along the road racing the setting sun.

Suddenly, he was there, stopping the procession, touching the bier. Why must there be such interruptions at times like this? Then she realized he was a stranger. His voice was reassuring, his prayer calm, his command so direct. "Young man, I tell you, arise!" (Luke 7:14).

Tears flow from joy as well as from grief. Her tears never stopped from the moment her son died till the moment the stranger gave him back to her alive. The joy she knew in that moment would not come to countless other women like herself. Their sons would go to war and never return. They would squander their inheritance in a restless pursuit of satisfaction at any cost. They would burn out their brains with drugs that promised a deeper experience of life but inevitably delivered the death blow sooner or later.

The joy of the widow of Nain is little comfort to those other women who meet no life-giving stranger along the road to the cemetery. He is not there for them to reverse the cruelty of such deaths. But, unseen, he does accompany them in their sadness, inviting them to find new strength in themselves and deeper faith in the resurrection life toward which all creation strains.

Prayer

*L*ORD, help me to comfort those who mourn the loss of their loved ones. Though no words of mine can take away that sadness, let me not run from their suffering but remain at their side as you would have me do.

SIMEON
Hope for the Future

"Now there was a man in Jerusalem whose name was Simeon. This man was righteous and devout, awaiting the consolation of Israel, and the holy Spirit was upon him" (Luke 2:25).

TO many of the inhabitants of Jerusalem, it was just an ordinary weekday at the Temple. Pilgrims from the surrounding towns of Judea climbed the magnificent staircase on the southern side of the courtyard along with visitors from Galilee who arrived at the Sacred Mount after long days of hard travel. The sight of the Temple and the fast pulse of life in the hilly streets nearby could always stir the imagination of the people from the country districts. The air was electric with the expectation that the Messiah when he came would certainly make his first public appearance in the City of the Great King, perhaps even within the Temple precincts.

SIMEON: HOPE FOR THE FUTURE

For the elderly Simeon, it was no ordinary day. There was a sense of urgency that made him hurry along through the crowds and the merchants whose donkeys reluctantly navigated the narrow streets with their heavy burdens. Despite the din of shopkeepers haggling over prices, Simeon was absorbed in the inspiration he had upon waking today. He sensed that today would bring the fulfillment of one of his most precious hopes. For many years, he had lived with a God-inspired conviction that he would see the Messiah within his own lifetime.

But how would Simeon recognize him? Would the Messiah have a large band of husky assistants to keep well-wishers in their place? Would the Messiah make his presence felt with a stirring denunciation of the Romans?

After so many years, so many centuries of waiting for the Messiah, the expectations of the people were too broad to be summed up in one person, even a person sent from God! Simeon's apprehension about recognizing the Messiah was well-founded.

But it all happened so simply—with the spontaneity so characteristic of the elderly who greet a young couple with a babe in arms. While other people might only see one more poorly dressed couple from the country carrying out their religious duties for a newborn boy, Simeon recognized the Messiah in a way others would have least expected.

The old man carried the child, but the child was the old man's Lord. The words came to his lips from somewhere deep inside his heart and the heart of his nation. "Now, Master, you may let your servant go in peace, according to your word, for my eyes have seen your salvation, which you prepared in the sight of all the peoples, a light for revelation to the Gentiles, and glory for your people Israel" (Luke 2:29-32).

God answered Simeon's prayer that day. Though Simeon would not live to see the revolution that this child would inaugurate, he had been blessed to know of its dawning. It would not be a revolution of armies and swords, but a warfare waged in the heart of humankind, a struggle for truth and justice, for holiness and true liberation of spirit as well as body.

Prayer

LORD, give me hope like Simeon. May it strengthen me against every obstacle.

☆ ☆ ☆

ANDREW
Leading Others to Christ

"Andrew, the brother of Simon Peter, was one of the two who heard John and followed Jesus. He first found his own brother Simon and told him, 'We have found the Messiah' " (John 1:40-41).

IN the Old Testament story of Cain's murder of his brother Abel, there is a classic line with which Cain tries to evade God's probing question "Where is Abel?" Cain vainly pretends innocence by replying "Am I my brother's keeper?" (Genesis 4:9). There is a great deal of Cain in many of us.

On the brighter side, how wonderful it is to hear the New Testament story of Andrew's genuine care and concern for his brother Simon. Andrew's conviction that he was his "brother's keeper" plays an essential role in this description of Simon Peter's call to discipleship.

The Synoptic Gospels generally picture Simon and Andrew as fishermen whom Jesus invited to leave their nets and become fishers of men. However, the Gospel according to John offers an entirely different picture. According to the Fourth Gospel, Andrew was already a disciple of John the Baptist. With another anonymous disciple, Andrew accepted the invitation of Jesus to "come and see" where he was dwelling. In the language of this Gospel, these words and gestures are highly significant of coming to faith in Christ. Through that encounter, Andrew became convinced that Jesus was the long-expected Messiah.

He could have kept this discovery to himself, but he did not. So deep was his conviction that he went home and brought his brother Simon to Jesus. The rest is history. Andrew slips into the shadows while Jesus builds his Church on Simon, whom Jesus nicknames Peter, or "Rocky."

No one of us comes to Christ alone. Even if it seems that Jesus entered our lives with the unpredictability of a lightning bolt on a cloudless day, most likely there is a Christian believer's influence somewhere else in our life. We all have people in our life who have been the midwife of our faith in

Christ. We all have a spiritual sister or brother who knew Christ before us, and who was so concerned about us that he/she made it possible for us to meet Jesus also. The rest is the history of our life in Christ.

Like Simon's Andrew, our own "Andrew" may have slipped quietly off the scene, perhaps in death or for some other reason. It does not matter. We are joined together with such persons for all eternity in the unbreakable bond of Christ's love from which nothing can separate us.

The question remains whether we have followed their example. Have we become an "Andrew" for someone else? Have we been our "brother's keeper" and brought someone to Christ?

Prayer

LORD Jesus, we thank you for the people in our lives who have been the instruments of your grace and peace. Enable us to be like Andrew through sharing our faith and bringing other people to know your power and love.

THE SAMARITAN WOMAN
Sharing Christ with Others

"Come see a man who told me everything I have done" (John 4:29).

LIFE was not always fair. She was not of the right stock, not of the purist Jewish clans. Yes, she had Semitic roots, but the geography was all wrong. Long ago there had been a great war in her district. Assyrian conquerors had brought in new people to mingle with the local residents. In that unfortunate shift of history, Jewish pedigree was lost forever. And some people have a way of never forgetting "bad blood." She was from the wrong side of the tracks, not entitled to sit at the great king's table for the heavenly banquet like the people born in Judea.

Love had not gone well either . . . a succession of partners who left her thirsting for something more substantial than tinkling jewelry and bright beads with flattery. Then, one day by the well came the stranger with the Galilean accent. She could see that he was tired and thirsty in the noonday heat, but he made the first move.

"Give me a drink" (John 4:7). He should not even have talked to her, for Jews used nothing in common with Samaritans. She hesitated—the conditioned reaction of a lifetime of being made to feel less than pure. But he went further, inviting her to ask for the living water he could give her. Yes, she would like to be free of the daily drudgery of coming to this well. "Sir, give me this water" (John 4:15).

Ah, but there's the rub. He was on a different wavelength. She would be most content to slake her physical thirst, but he insisted on moving to the level of the heart. "Go, call your husband and come back" (John 4:16). She made excuse. "I do not have a husband" (John 4:17). But this stranger was hard to fool. He knew her in ways she could not believe. The prophet, he must be the great teacher who would come. He even confirmed her suspicion. "I am he, the one who is speaking with you" (John 4:26).

How could this be? Dare she believe him? She must tell the others in town. "Could he possibly be the Messiah?" (John 4:29). They came, they heard for themselves, they believed. No longer was it her word alone, but she had been the messenger of Good News.

We like to say in the more democratic countries that people are born with certain rights of life, certain freedoms for self-initiative. In the more ancient cultures, it was not so. Clan and group were the yardstick of all possibility. Without them, an individual was in dire straits. But this Jewish prophet seemed more concerned about her than her pedigree or lack of it. He was not a messiah for the masses, but for each person one by one.

When Christ has touched our lives deeply, it is no surprise that we want to share that experience with others. We hesitate, at times, because they may think of us as mad or foolish. But the power of Christ's grace can overcome these quite natural human obstacles. If we are faithful to the experience, Christ can reach out to others through us.

Prayer

LORD, *refresh me with the living water of your wisdom and love. Make me courageous in letting others know what you mean to me.*

☆ ☆ ☆

PETER
Denial of Christ

"Peter stood at the gate outside. So the other disciple, the acquaintance of the high priest, went out and spoke to the gatekeeper and brought Peter in" (John 18:16).

THE woman was not usually wrong about voices. All these years of being gatekeeper at the high priest's house had taught her how to distinguish the accents of the Galilean northerners from the local clientele of Judea. Day in and day out, she had no end of opportunity to pick up the nuances of each region. You could bet on her every time, and no one ever questioned her judgment.

The Galilean preacher named Jesus was brought in rather abruptly late at night with much jostling and clanging of swords. Then, a little later, came the one who was known to the high priest. He was from Galilee, she was dead sure of that. He was probably raised near the lake since he had the mannerisms of a fisherman. She had noticed another companion who preferred to remain outside in the shadows of the alley. When the first fellow returned and asked her to let the outsider enter, it was only natural for her to ask him, "You are not one of this man's disciples, are you?" (John 18:17).

She must have struck a raw nerve in him to produce such a vehement denial. But she had learned to keep her place with such men. She knew they often exploded abusively when confronted with the truth about themselves. They were all bravado and blustering words of confidence on the surface, but when you looked into their eyes, you realized they were hoping the volume of their response would somehow increase the gullibility of the audience. They were usually running from someone or something, petrified that their trail might have been traced. This mysterious newcomer had that fearfulness about him. She was curious, but not so much that she would expose him to trouble.

She was even more convinced how right her intuition had been when he was asked the same thing twice again out in the courtyard and went through his denial routine, as if the practice would somehow make it more convincing.

Actually, she pitied him. He had nothing to fear from her but he was obviously tormented with fear for himself. She could understand him lying to save his own neck. She would not still be gatekeeper if she had not learned when to hold her tongue about what passed before her eyes day and night. Still, she wondered how he could find his own peace unless he stopped building it on a foundation of escape and denial.

Prayer

*L*ORD, *how often my own white lies and half-truths trip me up. I want peace in my life, but I do not always want to pay the price of truthfulness to achieve it. Give me the strength I need.*

NICODEMUS
Light out of Darkness

"Now there was a Pharisee named Nicodemus, a ruler of the Jews. He came to Jesus at night" (John 3:1-2).

THE dark of night serves as a cloak for many things. Thieves move about more freely, passions can be satisfied more spontaneously without fear of being recognized, even natural inhibitions tend to recede so that we dare to say and do things that mean the most to us in the white light of the moon or the yellow glare of a candle. People sometimes find the courage in the dark to blurt out the questions that haunt them during the day. Nicodemus came to Jesus at night. Perhaps he feared the harsh eye of his Pharisaic colleagues. Perhaps he only wanted to be sure that he would have the full attention of Jesus as he wrestled with making a decision about this preacher from Galilee. Or, just possibly, in John's poetic style, the dark night is not only outside of Nicodemus, but within him as well.

Jesus told him that he must be born again, born from above. We do not know Nicodemus' response to this nighttime revelation. For a while, we are left "in the dark," so to speak. But later, a most extraordinary thing happens.

Jesus was almost arrested at Jerusalem on the Feast of Tabernacles when his preaching led many to speculate that he might be the Messiah. The Pharisees dismissed this idea as something that only people with little concern for Jewish tradition would accept. At this point, when it was not fashionable to side with Jesus, Nicodemus spoke up. "Does our law condemn a person before it first hears him and finds out what he is doing?" (John 7:51). True, it is not a bold statement that would endanger Nicodemus too much. His concern for equal justice under the Mosaic law did not really implicate him in "the Jesus movement" that had been growing in the Galilee region. Such a statement would not make Nicodemus a martyr at the hands of his fellow dignitaries, but it must have caused them to wonder a bit about him. Was there a weak link in the chain of solidarity that their group was publicly manifesting against Jesus?

Nicodemus was beginning to take courageous steps, no longer hidden safely by night, but now in the sacred precincts where he spent his days with people of his own mindset. He was beginning to question their prejudice about Jesus. In the Gospel according to John, and actually in the constant teaching of Christian faith, the cross of Jesus remains the yardstick for distinguishing faith-filled disciples of the Son of Man.

At first, Nicodemus might have preferred a secure, private kind of socially approved religious practice, but he was a changed man. With Joseph of Arimathea, who had been a secret disciple for fear of the Jews, "Nicodemus, the one who had first come to him at night, also came bringing a mixture of myrrh and aloes weighing about one hundred pounds" (John 19:39). Commentators are quick to note the enormous quantity and value of these burial spices, an amount befitting a king. Nicodemus, the ruler, had been transformed into a servant of the Great King. The darkness had given way to the Light of the World. Is it possible that my secret name is Nicodemus?

Prayer

L ORD, when the going gets tough, you expect me to be tough enough to take the ridicule, even the condescending smiles of colleagues because I choose your standards as my own. Give me courage for today.

CONCLUSION

IN these passages, we have met a few of the biblical people whose stories are familiar to us. We have meditated on them in order to learn how their stories can give us insight as we write the story of our own lives day-by-day.

A beautiful song carefully and correctly printed in a song collection may be valuable and enriching to a trained musician who can appreciate the music without actually singing it aloud. However, the composer certainly wanted the song to come alive and fill the air so it could reach an audience without limits. Only then will that song affect us in one of the many ways that music moves the human spirit.

Likewise, these biblical stories may deeply touch us or inspire confidence in God in the privacy of our prayer. But they are meant to come alive again in the way we live out our commitment to the Lord.

Though some elements in the stories may seem far removed from the twentieth century, the virtues that these biblical characters exemplify are truly contemporary. By listening well, we take the first step in bringing these virtues to life in our own unique ways.